TABLE OF CONTENTS

Page

	Introduction	1
Chapter 1	Business, Industry, and Commerce	5
Chapter 2	Government and International Organizations	13
Chapter 3	Education	31
Chapter 4	Library Science	45
Chapter 5	Physical and Social Sciences	49
Chapter 6	Law	55
Chapter 7	Media	59
Chapter 8	Travel and Tourism	65
Chapter 9	Services	71
Chapter 10	Interpreting and Translating	79

APPENDIXES

Appendix A	Publications	89
Appendix B	1. Agencies and Organizations Concerned with Overseas Teaching and Research	91
	2. Sources of Information on Teaching Opportunities in Foreign Languages, TESOL, and Bilingual Education	92
Appendix C	Service Organizations	93
Appendix D	Associations of Translators and Interpreters	94

INDEX OF OCCUPATIONS

INTRODUCTION

The purpose of this book is to indicate fields in which people need foreign language skills in their work, and to provide suggestions and sources of further information for those who already have such skills or are planning to acquire them. The comments in the earlier editions about the value of foreign language proficiency in the world of work remain true, and should be emphasized even more strongly. In many fields the person with this ability has a definite advantage not only when competing for a job, but also in keeping up with world developments in that field.

For some positions, knowledge of at least one foreign language is a specific requirement. Increasingly, advertisements are being seen for executives, technicians and others "fluent in...." In many others, it is a valuable tool that is used regularly. In still others, it attests to the kind of international focus and skill development that employers seek, whether they need specific languages or not. It has even been said that during the next ten years a foreign language may be more helpful than a college diploma, given the undoubted international shape of tomorrow's world.

Foreign languages are important in careers because so many facets of American life—politics, media, the arts, science and technology, travel—have become truly international in scope. Furthermore, the involvement of American business in foreign countries, and of American citizens in foreign firms, is constantly expanding. Many U.S. corporations earn more than half of their profits overseas, and more and more Americans are finding jobs in this country as "local nationals" for foreign-owned companies. In this interdependent world, one out of six manufacturing jobs in the United States depends directly on foreign trade.

1

Yet American corporations are being forced to fill thousands of jobs abroad--including senior management positions--with citizens of other countries, partly because so few Americans have the requisite language skills. Similar deficiencies abound in government. For example, the National Council on Foreign Language and International Studies states that "the European division of the Office of the Secretary of Defense has some 80 employees who deal mainly with base site negotiations. None of the staff speaks German or French."

At the same time, the number of Americans whose native language is not English has grown dramatically. Spanish, for example, is no longer a "foreign" language but truly a "second" language in many parts of the country. In fact, the United States is now the fourth largest Spanish- speaking country in the world. In areas with large concentrations of such ethnic groups—including nearly every big city, and many towns and rural areas as well—a foreign language can prove useful in almost any job.

Countless surveys and even the most casual observation provide clear evidence that a knowledge of foreign languages enhances an individual's career prospects. As a complementary skill—in business, government service, law, education, the social and physical sciences, the media, the health professions—foreign language proficiency very often gives a crucial advantage in hiring and promotion.

Much has been written about why so many language-specific positions are not being filled by Americans, and why these opportunities are being lost. The President's Commission on Foreign Language and International Studies, in its 1979 report, documented the striking decline in language requirements and enrollment in recent decades. It strongly recommended that such requirements be reinstated, together with other measures. But more is needed. Language teachers themselves, as well as administrators and guidance counselors, must make students realize the possibilities open to those with language competence. If this is done properly, the motivation for language study might well make the imposition of requirements a secondary or even unnecessary solution.

In other words, neither students nor educators have fully recognized the career advantages that language proficiency offers. The author hopes that this book will help those possessing or acquiring foreign language competence, and their counselors and teachers, to become aware of the many and varied fields in which this skill comes into play.

Everything that has been said here about the value of languages in the business world, in government, and in the other career areas discussed applies not only to those who have learned them through study, but also—and most emphatically—to those who are bilingual because of their place of birth, family heritage or other circumstances. They possess a valuable resource, and should maintain and improve their foreign language competence in order to take full advantage of the opportunities they unquestionably enjoy.

●   ●   ●   ●   ●   ●

The response to the earlier editions of this book has been most gratifying to the author. Many of the schools and individuals who have used it as a career handbook have commented on its practical value to the student, teacher, counselor and job-hunter. It is hoped that this revised and expanded edition will prove equally valuable.

The author gratefully acknowledges the assistance of Martha Perrigaud in preparing this third edition.

Chapter 1

BUSINESS, INDUSTRY, AND COMMERCE

The connection between foreign languages and jobs in business and industry may not be obvious to those who assume that foreign languages are used only by translators, interpreters, and language teachers. Yet a survey of American business firms made by the Modern Language Association found that almost 70 percent do or could use personnel with language skills. In some cases a foreign language is required; in others it is very helpful. Many firms said that other things being equal, they give preference to the candidate who knows a foreign language. The combination of a foreign language and almost any other skill is therefore an excellent selling point for the job-hunter, and often increases the likelihood of finding interesting employment. In business and industry, the range of positions advertised week after week for which knowledge of a foreign language is required or desirable is broad and growing, and this trend can be expected to continue.

The reasons for this situation can be summarized briefly. With advances in transportation and communications and with expanding populations and markets, the interests of more and more firms—both here and abroad—have become international and even worldwide. The economic interdependence of nations is irreversible, and neither large nor small businesses can afford to ignore foreign possibilities. It is true that English is the most widely used language in international trade, but it is far from universal. Many times interpreters and other intermediaries, often engaged in the foreign country, must be used for business negotiations. The knowledge of foreign languages has become so important that many companies provide language training for their employees at the firm's expense. In some cases they would like to put Americans in key foreign positions, but are obliged to hire foreign nationals because of the language barrier.

Personnel with language skills are needed in many different types and places of work:

- Overseas, as agents and sales representatives of American firms doing business abroad;
- In the United States, as commercial representatives of foreign firms doing business here;
- In the overseas subsidiaries and affiliates of American firms in jobs at all levels from executive to clerical (tens of thousands of Americans are employed in such positions);
- In American branches of foreign firms;
- In the United States, by firms serving or employing members of non-English-speaking ethnic groups, especially the Hispanic community.

Clearly, graduates combining business and foreign languages will be able to market their skills. A recent survey showed that a majority of firms depend on outside services to identify and evaluate their overseas risks. Thus there are numerous career opportunities for graduates with skills in business and foreign languages, not only in the more traditional roles, but also with risk management groups in large corporations and private consulting firms.

In a tight job market, companies can afford to be more selective than ever, and the applicant who can offer a knowledge of foreign languages coupled with the necessary business skill has a clear advantage.

Managerial, executive, and marketing positions

The types of companies needing management and sales personnel with foreign language skills cover the whole spectrum of the business world. In their operations they find that foreign language proficiency is an enormous advantage in their home and overseas offices, and lack of it a real handicap. The following random selection of newspaper advertisements gives just an indication of the range of positions in which a foreign language is needed.

- Assistant to vice president for export operations (pharmaceuticals): "fluent Spanish required"
- Chief financial officer (retail chain based in southwestern United States): "fluency in Spanish required"
- International compensation specialist (computing equipment manufacturer): "fluency in a second language (French or Spanish) is most desirable"
- Assistant manager, accounting (importer of medical supplies): "knowledge of German helpful"
- Marketing research associate (pharmaceuticals): "familiarity with at least one foreign language"
- Systems analyst (consulting firm): "knowledge of Spanish essential"
- Contracts administrator (construction): "Italian/English fluency required"
- Sales manager (insurance company): "speak and write fluently in Spanish and English"
- Sales agent (real estate company): "bilingual"
- International sales engineer (electrical equipment manufacturer): "bilingual (Spanish/English) required"

Advertising is a field in which foreign language skills may be particularly useful. Knowledge of a culture and language can help avert ad translation blunders like "Corpse by Fisher" for "Body by Fisher" or the cultural myopia of a major aircraft company, which produced a slick brochure for an aircraft lift in India, only to discover that the turbans on the men pictured in the ad clearly indicated they were Pakistani.

Other positions for which companies find foreign language ability necessary or desirable include export manager, purchasing agent, overseas personnel manager, production manager, and marketing coordinator. Higher salaries and better promotion opportunities, as well as the initial advantage in consideration for many positions, are enjoyed by those with the requisite language skills.

Technical and engineering positions

Companies with overseas plants, those that manufacture machinery and equipment used abroad, American subsidiaries of foreign-based companies, manufacturers using foreign-made components in their U.S. operations—all are likely to need technical and engineering personnel with language proficiency. It is true that employees in these fields are seldom hired on the basis of language skill alone; yet, as an advertisement for an overseas plant manager stated, in seeking a qualified and experienced engineer, "knowledge of a foreign language is a definite plus." A petrochemicals company advertising for a process engineer to manage an overseas industrial complex (and offering a salary to $60,000) stated its preference for an individual with fluency in the local language. A firm seeking a transport equipment specialist offered an immediate position to a "French-speaking individual." Another firm advertised for an electronics engineer with at least five years' experience and "fluent in Mandarin Chinese and English." Knowledge of Spanish was specified in newspaper advertisements for telex/telegraph engineers, quality control supervisors, computer systems designers, production supervisors, and production engineers. Obviously, the value of U.S.-based technical employees selling or servicing equipment manufactured abroad is enhanced if they know the language of the country of origin. Locally, laboratory technicians, research workers, and technical writers can make excellent use of German, Japanese, and other languages to read material in their fields. Such people are not widely available in this country, and again the one who can offer a language skill in addition to technical qualifications has an evident edge.

Banking and financial positions

As international business and industry expand, international banking and financial activity naturally follows. Chase Manhattan Corporation recently had nearly half of its deposits in foreign branches. Today one fourth of all new direct investment goes abroad. This increased emphasis on the international financial market is accompanied by a growing need for auxiliary foreign language skills.

The variety of positions involved in this area is striking. A typical newspaper advertisement sought a controller for an industrial firm to be headquartered in New York City with about a third of the person's time devoted to travel in Latin America. The position, paying up to $45,000, required "bilingual skills in Spanish or Portuguese." An ad placed by a foreign-owned bank in California called for a senior credit analyst with a knowledge of French. A Miami-based international medical company was seeking a finance director for its branches in France and Germany. Other companies have advertised for auditors, accountants, banking correspondents, commercial loan officers, administrative assistants, domestic and international banking officers, and clerks—all requiring command of a foreign language. Banks with operations abroad need personnel able to communicate directly with clients in their own language. Likewise, local financial institutions that serve Spanish-speaking and other ethnic groups often hire bilingual officers, clerks, and tellers.

Secretarial and clerical positions

Bilingual secretaries are employed in virtually every area of activity from government to health institutions and universities. In the business world, the range of languages and fields is so vast that some employment agencies maintain permanent advertisements for bilingual typists and secretaries. Good typing, shorthand, and transcribing skills are essential, of course, and the lack of them will not be offset by the candidate's language ability. Another fact to be kept in mind is that the salaries advertised for bilingual secretaries are consistently higher than those for other secretarial positions. It is therefore well worthwhile for anyone planning to seek work of this kind to study a foreign language.

One reason why bilingual personnel are in such great demand in the secretarial and clerical area is that executives and managerial staff themselves often do not know the required languages and must hire assistants who do. Companies with overseas operations or affiliates, import-export firms, and banks are the most frequent employers of bilingual secretaries in the business sector. As at other levels, bilingual personnel are also sought by companies serving communities with sizable concentrations of minority groups.

The bilingual secretary has been described as a "stenographer, translator, and correspondent," which seems to broaden the range of duties considerably beyond that of a person without language ability, and this surely explains the salary premium enjoyed by bilingual personnel. In some companies the work may be highly specialized and limited only to foreign operations, such as the handling of foreign trade documents, invoices, and bills of lading. One firm advertised for a documents certification clerk with the ability to read Arabic; another needed an executive secretary fluent in German to deal with its major clients.

In addition to typist, stenographer, receptionist, and administrative secretary, the clerical fields open to bilingual personnel include some that might not be as readily apparent. For instance, a Washington, D.C. company sought a person fluent in Spanish and English to conduct telephone interviews. Switchboard operators, collection workers, and bookkeepers with language ability are also needed. Furthermore, the demand for such skills in secretarial and clerical work is not limited to any specific region of the country. Firms in southern states such as Georgia and South Carolina employ personnel with skills in German, French, and Spanish. In the West there is a large demand for Spanish-speaking secretarial staff in business and service fields and a growing need for secretaries with a good knowledge of Japanese. In the Minneapolis-St. Paul area, personnel directors indicated that command of a foreign language combined with typing, shorthand, accounting, and even drafting ability was a definite asset.

There are also opportunities for bilingual secretaries to work abroad in the foreign offices of American firms.

• • • • • •

Anyone interested in putting language skills to work in business or industry should certainly consult the classified advertisements in newspapers, magazines, and professional and trade publications, since these are the most direct means by which firms make their needs known. They may also suggest new ways in which job hunters can combine their foreign language ability with some other skill that would otherwise be less in demand. Even where a language requirement is not specifically stated, the candidate should make the prospective employer aware of this ability; an opportunity to make use of it may well arise in the future, either in the same position or in another job with the company.

Other sources of information are directories of American companies abroad, which can be found in most libraries; the *Occupational Outlook Handbook* of the Bureau of Labor Statistics, U.S. Department of Labor, which provides information on specific occupations; chambers of commerce and boards of trade; government and private employment agencies (the employer pays the fee for most overseas positions); and trade associations. Again, when contacting firms or agencies, the job seeker should list language ability as prominently as any other qualifications. A resourceful person may even see a need and propose being hired to fill it—such as bank teller, appliance salesman, or insurance agent in Spanish-speaking neighborhoods.

Special Note to Students

No one can tell you which language to study in order to get the best possible job. The languages most in demand are Spanish, French, and German, followed by Portuguese, Italian, Japanese, and Arabic. If you wish to offer one of these languages as an auxiliary skill, remember that the employer may well require fluency: ability to speak, read, and understand it easily, and possibly a knowledge of the technical or commercial vocabulary as well. The Labor Department's *Occupational Outlook Handbook*, mentioned above, surveys hundreds of occupations and provides information on many in which command of foreign language is necessary or useful. But bear in mind that most employers are not looking for translators, interpreters, or foreign language teachers. They need people who can fill a professional, technical, or clerical position as well as speak another language.

Among the specialized schools preparing people for bilingual careers in business and industry are:

- The *American Graduate School of International Management* (Glendale, AZ 85306), which trains college graduates for international careers. Its curriculum is taught by three interrelated departments: world business, international studies, and modern languages.
- The *Monterey Institute of International Studies* (425 Van Buren St., Monterey, CA 93940), which offers programs that reflect and address the needs arising from the ever-increasing interdependence of international economic activity. Students are prepared to work with sensitivity to cultures other than their own.

11

Chapter 2

GOVERNMENT AND INTERNATIONAL ORGANIZATIONS

One out of every six employed Americans is a civil servant, working for Federal, state, or local government. They hold a vast range of positions, from those unique to government (postal worker, police officer) to nearly every kind of job found in the private sector (doctor, accountant, teacher). In addition, many Americans are employed in professional as well as secretarial and clerical fields by international organizations of which the United States is a member. As in business and industry, language is most likely to be used as a supplement to other skills, except in language specialist positions such as translator and interpreter or in language teaching.

Federal Government

The Federal Government is the largest employer of Americans with foreign language skills, both in this country and abroad. Some agencies and departments have established "language essential" positions—but fewer than half are satisfactorily filled. This means greater opportunities for government employees with strong language capabilities.

About 90 percent of U.S. Government positions are under the Civil Service Act and Office of Personnel Management rules. The candidate for a specific job must obtain the announcement for that position, take the appropriate examination, and wait to be called. The announcement describes the position and requisite qualifications and tells the time and place of the examination. Selection is made from a list, on the basis of examination scores. Positions may call for research ability, a journalism or communications background, scientific and technical training, analytical or statistical skills, or knowledge of foreign affairs, as well as languages. United States citizenship is usually required.

The benefits of Federal employment are well known and include liberal leave provisions (annual and sick leave), low-cost life and medical insurance, transportation to and from foreign posts, a guaranteed pension, job protection, and equal opportunity for promotion.

The following is a general survey of United States Government departments and agencies that require personnel with language skills. To obtain announcements for specific positions, or for other information, write United States Office of Personnel Management, Washington, D.C. 20415 or contact the nearest Federal Job Information Center.

Department of State

The Department of State employs 15,000 Americans around the world. In Washington, personnel work on political, economic, social, and labor affairs, research, public affairs, and diplomatic and consular matters. The Department has stated that in the field of foreign affairs it is placing increased emphasis on the language capability of its Foreign Service Officers. Under exchange and technical assistance programs with other countries, the expert in almost any field who has mastered a foreign language will have a decided advantage over similarly trained experts who lack this ability. The Department's Foreign Service Institute provides language instruction to staff members, using native speakers as teachers.

Foreign Service Officers (FSOs) staff over 300 United States diplomatic and consular offices around the world, and serve in Washington as well. A Department of State handbook points out that officers are expected to acquire an acceptable level of proficiency in at least one foreign language.

FSOs receive special training after entering the Department. They are assigned duties in the economic, business, political, and cultural areas; they serve as consular officers and in administrative positions. Overseas, they have

14

extensive contact with foreigners, interpreting United States foreign policy, protecting the interests of Americans abroad, processing visas, and carrying on intelligence work. To qualify for appointment the candidate must pass the Foreign Service examination, have a degree, be at least 21 and a U.S. citizen, and pass a rigid physical examination and a security investigation. Names of qualified applicants are placed on a register from which appointments are made as the need arises. There are special recruitment programs for the hiring of women and minorities.

The State Department's Language Services Division employs a number of translators and interpreters, both on its permanent staff and under short-term contracts (See Chapter 10).

(Employment Division, Department of State, Washington, D.C. 20520)

Agency for International Development (AID)

AID, a semi-autonomous agency within the U.S. International Development Cooperation Agency, administers the majority of United States aid to over 60 countries. The agency provides technical assistance to less developed countries. Its overseas employees hold professional and technical positions in agriculture, finance, education, engineering, housing, communications media, industry, labor, public health, and transportation. Positions include accountant, auditor, budget analyst, business analyst, information officer, loan officer and personnel specialist. Specialized experience is required for most operational positions, which are of three types:

- *Interns* work in such areas as accounting, management, economics, and public administration. Candidates must have a degree and some experience in the relevant field, as well as U.S. citizenship and good health.
- *Mid-level appointees* have substantial formal education or the work equivalent, plus several years of professional experience.
- *Senior staff* have specialized work experience and a strong academic background, often a doctorate.

The most frequent needs are for economists, financial analysts, staff attorneys, auditors and accountants, to work in Washington, D.C. and the Agency's overseas missions.

Although more than half of AID's employees use foreign languages, the agency has no official language requirements. French, Spanish, and Portuguese are the most practical, but personnel are encouraged to learn Arabic and other less common languages for work in specific countries.
(Office of Personnel Management, Agency for International Development, Washington, D.C. 20523)

United States Information Agency (USIA)

USIA employs over 2,000 persons with skills in some 50 languages, at posts around the world. The agency maintains information offices and libraries in many countries, and operates the Voice of America radio network. Many positions are filled by Foreign Service Officers, and there are also non-career openings in clerical, library, radio, and administrative work. Temporary employment is available to professionals such as lawyers, teachers, and agricultural specialists.

USIA also hires guides who are fluent in the language of the host country to take part in Agency exhibits in Eastern Europe, the Soviet Union and other locations. These are temporary positions lasting from one to seven months, depending upon the duration of the exhibit. Guides have excellent opportunities to travel, improve their language skills and enjoy contact with people of other cultures.

In addition to operating its libraries and reading rooms, USIA publishes magazines in English and foreign languages for distribution abroad. It also acquires or produces a variety of media products for use by USIA overseas posts. Besides the fields already mentioned, these operations require experts on the customs and cultures of other nations, social science analysts, public information officers, and printers. The languages in greatest demand are French and Spanish.

USIA also works with *Binational Centers*, which are autonomous local organizations dedicated to the development of mutual understanding between the United States and the host country. In some cases, a center may be directed by a USIA officer, but most centers are independent of USIA assistance except for occasional program collaboration. Typical activities include English classes, lectures, film presentations and art exhibits. Hiring for most positions at the centers is done at the local level. A list of binational centers and an information sheet on English teaching positions abroad may be obtained from the Office of Cultural Centers and Resources, USIA, 301 4th St., S.W., Washington, D.C. 20547.

The *Voice of America* (VOA) radio service broadcasts news, educational, entertainment, and other programs in many languages. Candidates for VOA positions must have a college degree plus skills in communications, journalism, foreign affairs, government, and/or related social sciences. Fluency in the language is a must; a near-perfect accent ("native fluency") and a good speaking voice are required for announcers. The work, in Washington and abroad, includes writing, editing, translating, reporting special events, evaluating material for broadcast use, and production.

(Employment Branch, Office of Personnel, United States Information Agency, Washington, D.C. 20547)

Peace Corps

The Peace Corps, formerly a component of ACTION, was established as an independent agency in 1981.

The aims of the Peace Corps are to help developing nations meet their needs for trained personnel and to promote mutual understanding between Americans and the people of those countries. Over 5,000 volunteers serve in 58 countries throughout the world.

In general, the Peace Corps can use volunteers with almost any background or combination of experience and education. Volunteers with degrees and/or training in the following areas are needed:

- life and environmental sciences
- forestry
- fisheries
- agriculture
- architecture and city planning
- science
- engineering
- industrial arts
- business and finance
- health professions
- homemakers/home economists
- educators
- math/science specialties

- generalists—those with degrees in liberal arts and social work, or experienced in home management or handicrafts, etc.

Peace Corps volunteers must know or be trained in the language of the country where they are assigned. Appointment is open to U.S. citizens of all ages who have the requisite skills and experience and meet legal and medical criteria. Applicants with dependents are not taken. Training, which lasts from 9 to 14 weeks and is often given in the host country, emphasizes cultural studies as well as the local language. Volunteers are also trained in teaching techniques, health and medicine, and physical education and recreation. A monthly allowance is paid in local currency for food, lodging, and incidentals, enabling the volunteer to live at the local standard of living. Free medical care is provided. A readjustment allowance is set aside in the United States, usually payable upon completion of service.

ACTION

The VISTA (Volunteers in Service to America) program, administered by ACTION, responds to needs identified by communities in the United States, providing full-time volunteers for projects sponsored by local nonprofit organizations. VISTA is active both in cities and in rural areas. Volunteers include community advocates, crafts people, health workers, business specialists, teachers, architects, and lawyers. Some are recruited in the local community by the sponsoring organization, while others are recruited throughout the country and assigned to projects where their services have been requested. Projects include community development, health services, economic development, energy-related matters, housing, legal rights, and education.

VISTA volunteers with a knowledge of Spanish, French, or Indian languages are needed for projects involving those ethnic groups. The minimum age is 18; there is no upper limit. A college degree is not required, and volunteers have a wide variety of backgrounds.

(ACTION, Personnnel Management Division, Washington, D.C. 20525)

Department of Agriculture

The *Foreign Agricultural Service* (FAS) of the Agriculture Department is an export promotion and service agency for U.S. agriculture. It assigns attaches to about 70 overseas posts, usually on a rotating basis from Washington. The Service administers international marketing agreements and commodity programs, and carries out economic and agricultural research and reporting. In general, it represents U.S. agricultural interests abroad.

Agricultural attaches are assigned to major agricultural consuming and marketing areas of the world. While a foreign language is not an absolute recruiting requirement, its value for the job is recognized and language familiarity is given consideration. Knowledge of the local language is a prerequisite for service in many posts. Language training is provided and intensive training prior to actual assignment is customary.

FAS also recruits U.S. citizen candidates for positions in international organizations, such as the Food and Agriculture Organization of the United Nations, whose activities are concerned with agriculture. During international negotiations, FAS provides staff and support for U.S. representation.

The *Office of International Cooperation and Development* (OICD) plans and directs the efforts of the Department of Agriculture in international development and technical cooperation, including international cooperative research. In this office an estimated 25% of the staff use language skills in French, Spanish and Chinese on the job.

The *Farmers Home Administration* provides loans and grants for agricultural development. It has local offices throughout most of the United States. Knowledge of Spanish would be especially helpful to personnel assigned to county offices which serve areas with Hispanic populations.

(Office of Personnel, Department of Agriculture, Washington, D.C. 20250)

Department of Commerce

The Department's *International Trade Administration* (ITA) administers the Foreign Commercial Service, whose personnel monitor and report to government and the public on

19

commercial, market, and economic developments around the world. Each officer is responsible for a specific country or area. Knowledge of the relevant language is obviously desirable for such positions, together with a general background in economics, marketing, business administration, or statistics. Other positions in which foreign language proficiency would be helpful are in export development offices, formerly known as trade centers, which are maintained by ITA in many of the major industrialized countries.

The *Bureau of the Census* hires advisers in statistics to work abroad in technical assistance programs. Academic training in statistics and economics is required. Analysts in the fields of demography, economics, and finance work on publications exchanges and reports dealing with foreign statistics.

The *United States Travel Service* is charged with promoting travel from foreign countries to the United States. Employees of its six offices overseas must be fluent in the language of the country to which they are assigned, and possess appropriate experience and academic training in international sales and promotion including advertising, international economics, marketing and market research, business administration, and public relations.

The *National Oceanic and Atmospheric Administration* (NOAA) maintains weather stations in places outside the contiguous United States, including Puerto Rico, Mexico and the Pacific Islands. Meteorologists, electronics specialists, and research scientists working at such stations would find familiarity with the local language useful at the very least. Foreign language research skills may also be useful in NOAA's research programs, areas that include marine and atmospheric sciences, solar-terrestrial physics, experimental meteorology, and satellite observation of the environment.

Other Commerce Department offices that may need personnel with language skills include the National Bureau of Standards, Patent and Trademark Office, National Technical Information Service, and Minority Business Development Agency.

(Office of Personnel, Department of Commerce, Washington, D.C. 20230)

Department of Energy

The *International Affairs Office* is responsible for developing and managing programs related to international aspects of energy policy. Members of this office travel extensively in order to assess energy trends throughout the world and participate in programs with other countries and multinational organizations. Knowledge of a foreign language, particularly French or Spanish, would be most useful in this branch of the Department.

(Office of Personnel, Department of Energy, Washington, D.C. 20585)

Department of Defense

The three services (Army, Navy, Air Force) require personnnel with foreign language ability to deal with military affairs involving foreign countries. Many of the fields are highly technical.

The *Defense Intelligence Agency* employs economists, geologists, translators, engineers, and meteorologists in its intelligence-gathering work. In a recent newspaper advertisement the Agency sought bilingual research technicians for diverse clerical and administrative duties: reviewing foreign newspapers and documents, translating, typing, preparing briefs and abstracts. Fluency was required.

The *National Security Agency*, which functions under the Department of Defense, employs research assistants, communications experts, and translators, all of whom must know foreign languages. This agency makes its appointments independently of civil service regulations. Applicants must be native-born United States citizens. A background in international affairs, economics, psychology, history, or sociology, combined with a major or minor in foreign languages, is desirable. The need is greatest for Eastern European, Arabic, and Far Eastern languages.

The *Defense Language Institute* employs teachers for its courses in many foreign languages and dialects (See Chapter 3).

(Directorate for Personnel and Security, Washington Headquarters Services, Department of Defense, Washington, D.C. 20301)

Central Intelligence Agency (CIA)

The CIA is the primary intelligence-gathering arm of the United States Government. It employs U.S. citizens with backgrounds in international relations, political science, economics, history, geography, engineering, physics, and chemistry, as well as foreign languages. The requirements for the CIA's foreign publications monitoring positions are a thorough command of the written language, a good educational background, and knowledge of current international affairs. Oral comprehension is also desirable. Russian, Eastern European, Middle Eastern and Oriental languages are in greatest demand, although Romance languages in combinations of two or more are acceptable. These personnel scan foreign books, newspapers, and periodicals for information needed by foreign policy analysts and policy makers. In 1981 the CIA's second-ranking official told a Congressional panel that CIA operations had been severely hampered by a shortage of qualified linguists. Indeed, the CIA recently listed "the ability to speak or to learn a foreign language" among its qualifications for work with the agency. There is some opportunity for overseas service, but most CIA positions are located in Washington.

(Office of Personnel, Central Intelligence Agency, Washington, D.C. 20505)

Department of Education

The *Office of International Education* sponsors various programs in this country and abroad for advanced research and study in modern foreign languages. A knowledge of foreign languages and cultures is necessary for those who work in developing and administering programs, which include the Teacher Exchange Program (in cooperation with the U.S. Information Agency), International Studies Centers, Foreign Language and Area Studies Fellowships, Research Programs, Graduate and Undergraduate International Studies Programs, and the Foreign Curriculum Consultant Program. (For specific program information, contact the Office of International Education).

The *Office of Bilingual Education* ensures access to equal educational opportunity and improves the quality of programs for limited English proficiency and minority language populations. The working language of the agency is obviously English, but about half the employees speak a foreign language.

(Office of Personnel, U.S. Department of Education, Washington, D.C. 20202)

Department of the Interior

As the nation's principal conservation agency, the Department of the Interior is responsible for most of our nationally owned public lands and natural resources. At the bureau level of the Department, which includes the Bureau of Mines, Geological Survey, Fish and Wildlife Service, National Park Service, Bureau of Reclamation, and Bureau of Land Management, experts are often sent on short-term consulting assignments around the world. These missions are generally arranged and paid for by AID. Here again, language is not a prerequisite for hiring, but a spokesman for the Department of the Interior terms it "very useful."

People working for the *Indian Affairs Office* of the Department would find their field of work, for example social services or law enforcement, facilitated by a knowledge of Indian languages, and in fact there are employees familiar with Indian languages throughout that office.

(Office of Personnel, Department of the Interior, Washington, D.C. 20240)

Department of Justice

The *Federal Bureau of Investigation* (FBI) employs linguists and also makes use of the language skills of its special agents.

The *Drug Enforcement Administration* (DEA) conducts domestic and international investigations of major drug traffickers, cooperating with Federal and local agencies as well as foreign governments. It provides special training in narcotic and dangerous drug control to United States and foreign law enforcement officers. DEA employs Americans fluent in the languages of the countries where they are assigned.

The *Immigration and Naturalization Service* (INS) is responsible for administering the laws relating to the admission, exclusion, deportation, and naturalization of aliens. Through its offices in the United States and abroad it provides information to those seeking U.S. citizenship. INS personnel conduct investigations, detect violations of the immigration laws, and determine the suitability of aliens to enter the United States. They need a knowledge of the foreign language involved, together with the appropriate background in law enforcement and related fields. Border patrol officers use Spanish and many other languages.

The *International Affairs Office* of the *Criminal Division is* charged with drawing up and carrying out transnational criminal justice enforcement policies, including international extradition and mutual legal assistance. Attorneys in this office find language skills helpful and even necessary, as they deal personally with representatives of foreign governments. An office spokesman says that all other factors being equal, an attorney fluent in a foreign language would be hired over one lacking skills in that area.

(Personnel Office, Department of Justice, Washington, D.C. 20530)

Department of Labor

The *Bureau of International Labor Affairs* helps formulate international economic and trade policies affecting American workers. It also helps represent the United States in multilateral and bilateral trade negotiations, and in international organizations such as the General Agreement on Tariffs and Trade. The Bureau carries out overseas technical assistance projects and arranges trade union exchange and other programs for foreign visitors to the United States. The languages most emphasized in these programs are Spanish and French.

The *Bureau of Labor Statisics*, which is responsible for the Department's economic and statistical research activities, collects data on the international aspects of labor economics.

Both of these bureaus have some requirement for economists, statisticians, and other specialists with language proficiency. European and Far Eastern languages are needed in the statistical field.

(Reception and Correspondence Unit, Department of Labor, Washington, D.C. 20210)

Department of the Treasury

The *Office of the Assistant Secretary (International Affairs)* assists in the formulation and execution of international financial, economic, commercial, energy, and trade policies and programs. It employs specialists in these fields for research on conditions in other countries, coordination of bilateral and multilateral programs, and relations with foreign governments and international agencies.

The *U.S. Customs Service* collects revenue from imports and administers customs and related laws. It works closely with international organizations and foreign customs services. Some personnel are stationed overseas, making use of German, French, Spanish, Chinese, and other languages.

(Office of Personnel, Department of the Treasury, Washington, D.C. 20220)

Smithsonian Institution

The *Smithsonian Institution,* founded in 1846 for the "increase and diffusion of knowledge," publishes the results of studies, preserves over 78 million items of scientific, cultural and historical interest, and maintains exhibits devoted to American history, technology and aeronautics. It also conducts education programs and national and international cooperative research and training. Foreign language skills are useful in the Offices of International Activities, Folklife Programs, Museum Programs, International Exchange Service, and others.

(Office of Personnel, Smithsonian Institution, Washington, D.C. 20560)

Library of Congress

Personnel of the Library of Congress utilize foreign languages in a wide range of activities: acquisition, cataloging and classification, reference, and research. The Library uses over 450 languages in connection with its more than 19 million books and pamphlets, the majority of which are in non-English languages.

Among the Library departments most in need of language skills are the Department of Research Services (organized in area-specific units including the African and Middle East, Asian, European, and Hispanic Divisions); the Congressional Research Service; the Law Library, which is involved in the study of law in many languages; and others.

While a degree in library science is especially important in the Library's processing services and administrative units, most of the staff performing research have other academic training in addition to the required language capabilities.

(Recruitment and Placement Office, Library of Congress, Washington, D.C. 20540)

• • • • • •

Other U.S. Government agencies in which a knowledge of foreign languages would be desirable include:

Automated Data and Telecommunications Service
Export-Import Bank of the United States
Federal Communications Commission
Foreign Claims Settlement Commission
Inter-American Foundation
National Aeronautics and Space Administration
Overseas Private Investment Corporation
Trade and Development Program
U.S. International Trade Commission

The purposes and programs of most Federal Government agencies are described in the *United States Government Manual* published by the General Services Administration. It is available in libraries or from the Superintendent of Documents, U.S. Government Printing Office, Washington, D.C. 20402.

Local Government

In areas where large numbers of citizens do not speak English, local governments need employees with foreign language skills. The extent to which foreign languages are used depends on the ethnic makeup of the community. In any area with sizable concentrations of minority or immigrant groups there will be some positions for which languages are required and others where they would be a definite advantage.

Some cities and states have offices of bilingual programs which carry out and oversee special programs for such groups. Social workers, counselors, home economists, and education specialists are often hired to serve Spanish-speaking residents. In New York City the police find Spanish highly useful—over 500 police officers enroll each semester in Spanish courses offered by the City University of New York. Large concentrations of Spanish-speaking people can be found in many other cities, including Miami, Washington, Chicago, and Los Angeles. The situation has made bilingual or multilingual speakers "extremely important" to police, according to Arlington, Virginia Police Chief William Stover. He said his department has had to give knowledge of foreign languages great consideration in hiring. With the recent influx of Asian immigrants, a knowledge of any of the Oriental languages would be highly useful in working with members of those groups.

International Organizations

The United States participates in many international organizations, some of which have their headquarters in this country. These organizations usually offer employment to nationals of any member country, in professional, clerical, and language specialist positions. The policy of geographical balance in staffing limits the number of openings for United States citizens. In this country, about 25 percent of the positions in each organization are held by Americans.

The following is a brief description of the largest international organizations with headquarters in the United States. It should be kept in mind that qualified U.S. citizens are eligible for employment in these or in any other such organization in which the United States participates. For a complete listing, see the *Yearbook of International Organizations* available in many college and public libraries. The *Yearbook* lists thousands of governmental and private international organizations, their structure and aims, and their members. The *United States Government Manual* mentioned above also contains a listing and brief description of selected international organizations.

United Nations (UN)

The purposes of the United Nations are to maintain international peace and security, to develop friendly relations among nations, and to achieve international cooperation in solving economic, social, cultural, and humanitarian problems. The worldwide interests of the UN demand a broad range of skills and abilities. It employs professional economists, education specialists, financial analysts, public information officers, librarians, technical specialists in industry and agriculture, engineers, and statisticians. The UN is the largest employer of language specialists—translators, editors, interpreters—in this country (See Chapter 10). In addition, the organization has a continuing need for clerical and secretarial staff, preferably bilingual. The official languages of the UN are English, French, Spanish, Arabic, Russian, and Chinese, so that English combined with any of the others would be required.

Many Americans are also employed in professional positions by the specialized agencies of the United Nations, including:

Food and Agriculture Organization
International Labor Organization
International Telecommunications Union
United Nations Educational, Scientific, and Cultural
  Organization
World Health Organization
World Metereological Organization
(Personnel Office, United Nations, New York 10017)

Organization of American States (OAS)

The OAS is the regional organization of Western Hemisphere nations. Its secretariat in Washington provides technical and administrative services to the OAS councils, to inter-American programs, and to the member countries. The staff includes specialists in economics, finance, business administration, statistics, accounting, law, community development, cooperatives, and taxation, as well as language specialists. Clerical positions are also open to U.S. citizens. A knowledge of two or more of the Organization's official languages (English, French, Spanish, and Portuguese) is required.

(Personnel Office, Organization of American States, 17th Street and Constitution Avenue N.W., Washington, D.C. 20006)

World Bank and International Monetary Fund

The World Bank, an intergovernmental organization with more than 140 members, assists in the development of its member countries by making loans for productive purposes and promoting private investment through guarantees and participations. In its work the Bank requires financial analysts, loan officers, project analysts, lawyers, economists, statisticians, translators and interpreters, and specialists in agriculture, rural and urban development, civil engineering, and industry, as well as administrative and clerical personnel.

The International Monetary Fund is similar to the World Bank in its structure, though it has a smaller staff. The Fund promotes international monetary cooperation and exchange stability, providing foreign exchange to its members for balance of payments support. It serves as a mechanism for consultation and cooperation and monitors the international financial situation. The staff includes specialists in finance, law, economics, accounting, and statistics, as well as language specialists and support and clerical personnel.

The official language of both the World Bank and the International Monetary Fund is English, but the scope of their operations makes knowledge of a foreign language necessary for some positions, and desirable for many others. Competition for professional positions is keen, and many if not most applicants have advanced degrees.

(Personnel Department, World Bank, Washington, D.C. 20433; Personnel Department, International Monetary Fund, Washington, D.C. 20431)

Inter-American Development Bank (IDB)

The IDB is the regional development bank for the Western Hemisphere, resembling the World Bank in its organization and functions. A knowledge of Spanish and/or Portuguese is needed for most positions at all levels. The professional fields of IDB staff members are the same as those of the World Bank.

(Personnel Department, Inter-American Development Bank, 808 17th Street, N.W., Washington, D.C. 20577)

Pan American Health Organization (PAHO)

The purposes of this organization are to support and coordinate efforts of the Western Hemisphere countries to combat disease, lengthen life, and promote physical and mental health. Its activities include training of health workers, eradication and control of communicable diseases, water supply and environmental sanitation, and reduction of nutritional deficiencies. PAHO employs health specialists in all fields, as well as administrative and clerical staff. A knowledge of Spanish or Portuguese is highly desirable or required for many positions, especially those in the field.

(Personnel Department, Pan American Health Organization, 525 23rd Street, N.W., Washington, D.C. 20037)

References

How to Get a Job in the Federal Government,
prepared by the Office of Personnel Management, 1983.

United States Government Manual,
prepared by the General Services Administration, latest edition.

Yearbook of International Organizations,
latest edition.

Chapter 3

EDUCATION

Education is one of the largest "industries" in the United States, involving 49 million elementary and secondary pupils and 8 million college students. In 1983 nearly 3 million full-time teachers were employed in the nation's elementary and secondary schools and colleges and universities. Some teach part-time, especially at the post-secondary level; among them are many scientists, physicians, accountants, members of other professions, and graduate students. Still others teach in preschool and adult education and recreation programs.

There are three major facets of education: research, administration (including counseling), and teaching. Knowledge of a foreign language can be important in all three areas.

Research

The importance of foreign languages in academic research is demonstrated by the fact that many master's degree and doctoral programs require some foreign language study. A great deal of original research material as well as reports of prior research are available only in languages other than English. Persons engaged in research need at least a functional knowledge of the languages relevant to their work. In fields such as sociology, anthropology, religion, political science, and comparative literature, the need is self-evident. For those involved in the sciences it is no less real: in meteorology, physics, geology, mathematics, chemistry, and the biological sciences, up to 30 percent of published research is in Russian, and nearly 15 percent in French or German. Translation bureaus exist, but they do not translate all the material available and generally provide only abstracts of articles. Obviously, the researcher who can make use of foreign language material will be able to do much more with his or her subject and will be in a better position than colleagues who cannot.

The U.S. Department of Education conducts programs both within the United States and abroad for individuals and groups to carry out basic and applied research in international and intercultural studies. Participants include college, secondary, and elementary school teachers, as well as curriculum supervisors and administrators. The purpose of these research programs is to develop curricula and instructional materials related to foreign language and area studies. Comparative education studies on the educational systems of other countries are also sponsored.

Administration and Counseling

In the fields of educational administration and counseling, foreign languages are likely to be of direct importance for those who come in contact with non-English-speaking students or community and parents' groups. Particularly in counseling, there is an ever-greater need for people at both the college and secondary levels who can assist the growing number of foreign students and members of Hispanic and other ethnic groups now in American schools. Traditionally, it has not been necessary for administrative personnel to learn the languages of parents and students; school was the institution that "socialized" students away from their ethnic cultures into the mainstream, English-speaking culture. Increasingly, however, schools are being asked to help preserve ethnic cultures in America, and to be more aware of the needs of those who do not speak English. In such situations, a knowledge of foreign languages will help administrators and counselors to be more effective.

One sign of this trend is the proliferation of bilingual schools and academies, where bilingual persons specially trained in linguistics and education teach English to students who speak other languages. Administrative personnel are needed for supervision and curriculum development in such schools.

Advisory and administrative personnel are also needed overseas. The U.S. Department of Education refers highly experienced and specialized American citizens as candidates in an international selection process for posts in the UNESCO technical assistance program in developing countries. The need is greatest for (1) experts with prior professional experience in teacher education, curriculum development, science education, and national educational planning; and (2) specialists in educational innovation, technology, and media. Candidates generally are required to have an advanced degree and five to ten years of specialized experience. The U.S. Agency for International Development also sends education specialists abroad, usually to work as advisers or administrators.

Department of Defense Dependents Schools, located in 22 countries around the world, are staffed with administrative and support personnel recruited in the United States. These professionals generally deal with English- speaking students, but knowledge of a foreign language enables them to deal with the community more effectively and to benefit fully from their time abroad.

Teaching

This section deals primarily with teaching positions for which knowledge of a foreign language is required in addition to preparation in other academic fields. The teaching of foreign languages as an academic subject and teaching of English as a foreign language will be discussed in the following section.

Recent legislation in the field of bilingual education has increased the demand for teachers fluent in a second language. At present, bilingual education programs in the United States are primarily for students who do not speak English as their native language. By presenting lessons in the home language, bilingual education gives students with little or no proficiency in English the opportunity to realize their academic potential. Information on these positions is available from the National Clearinghouse for Bilingual Education (See Appendix B for address).

There are many opportunities for teachers with foreign language skills abroad, where they teach English, American civilization, and other subjects on an exchange basis or through direct placement. Those who can show competence in English as well as in the language of the foreign country should find positions available. For the teacher going overseas, college training should have included methods of teaching English as a foreign language, area studies, and international relations. At least a college minor in the field to be taught is usually required, together with a background knowledge of the local and American cultures. The American teacher employed abroad will be asked penetrating questions on United States institutions, customs, geography, history, and government; he or she should be as well informed on these subjects as possible.

One of the most useful publications on teaching and other opportunities overseas in the field of education is *Study and Teaching Opportunities Abroad,* prepared by the Department of Education. It is available for $4.50 from the Superintendent of Documents, U.S. Government Printing Office, Washington, D.C. 20402 (Stock No. 017-080-02063-7). This booklet lists and describes many educational positions overseas, indicates the sponsoring agencies, and gives addresses for obtaining further information.

Fulbright-Hays Program

Under the Fulbright-Hays Act, opportunities are provided for elementary and secondary school teachers and college instructors and professors to teach in foreign elementary and secondary schools and colleges. The American teacher may participate in a direct exchange of positions with a teacher from abroad or may simply be placed in a foreign school. Teachers of English as a foreign language are eligible to participate. The applicant must have a least a bachelor's degree, be a U.S. citizen, and have three years of teaching experience, preferably in the subject field and at the level for which application is made. The work may also include curriculum development and preparation of teaching materials. Seminars abroad are also funded by this program. Information and application materials may be obtained from the Teacher Exchange Section of the U.S. Department of Education (See Appendix B for address).

The Institute of International Education administers Fulbright-Hays grants as well as grants offered by foreign governments, universities, foundations and private donors. It provides information on foreign study opportunities, undergraduate and graduate programs sponsored by U.S. colleges and universities, and teaching opportunities abroad (See Appendix B for address).

In cooperation with other agencies, the Council for International Exchange of Scholars also helps administer the Fulbright-Hays program. Opportunities are available in post-secondary institutions for both lecturing and research. Basic eligibility requirements include U.S. citizenship, post-doctoral teaching experience at the appropriate level, or recognized professional credentials (these can include faculty rank or publications, compositions, exhibitions, etc.). Although some awards require no foreign language ability, the majority rate such knowledge as "helpful", "useful", "required" or "essential" (See Appendix B for address).

U.S. Government Positions

Teaching opportunities overseas are available within several branches of the Federal Government. The Army, Navy, and Air Force operate schools abroad, known as Overseas Dependents Schools, for the children of their personnel stationed in foreign countries. These Department of Defense schools offer an opportunity for teachers to utilize and perfect their language ability while living and working in a particular country. Courses of study parallel those of the public schools in the United States, and standard approved textbooks are used. Some of the elementary schools are small, and the teacher must teach multiple grades. Many junior high schools have only four to eight teachers, and each one may be required to teach two or more different subjects. Secondary teachers are also required to teach in more than one field and should be prepared to conduct at least one extracurricular activity. United States citizenship, good physical condition and mental stability, and availability for worldwide placement are prerequisites. Appropriate academic preparation and certification also are necessary.

Information is available from Overseas Dependents Schools, Department of Defense (See Appendix B for address).

Peace Corps volunteers teach in elementary, secondary, normal and vocational schools in many countries. There is a great need for teachers of English, as well as for experienced mathematics and science teachers. Volunteers work in Africa, the Near East, Latin America, Southeast Asia, and the Pacific. The aims and programs of the Peace Corps are described more fully in Chapter 2.

Information about the Federal Government teaching positions mentioned above may be obtained from the sources listed in Appendix B.

Other teaching positions abroad

The National Education Association maintains a Teacher Exchange Computer Listing for its members through the Office of International Relations. Interested teachers are matched with others in similar positions by grade level and subject taught. Although the majority of exchanges are domestic, some international possibilities exist. The Association's Office of International Relations and Peace Programs also distributes a free resource guide to overseas opportunities for travel, study, exchanges and employment (See Appendix B for address).

There are teaching positions in other American-sponsored overseas elementary and secondary schools which are assisted by the Department of State. Employment opportunities should be investigated by writing directly to each school's chief administrator. A list of such schools may be obtained from the Office of Overseas Schools, U.S. Department of State (See Appendix B for address). The International Education Programs Office of the Department of Education furnishes information about teaching in United States territories.

Volunteers are placed in elementary to university level positions in schools around the world by religious organizations. The objectives of such programs include assisting young people and adults in developing areas, either within formal educational systems or in alternative ways.

University lecturing and research appointments abroad are open to United States citizens with a doctoral degree and appropriate experience. Most academic fields are acceptable. Travel-only grants and grants for lecturing and research for younger scholars who have at least a master's degree are also available. Inquiries may be sent to the Council for International Exchange of Scholars (See Appendix B for address).

36

An agency that recruits teachers, administrators, librarians and curriculum specialists for positions in schools overseas serving the American and international communities is International Schools Services (see Appendix B for address).

The Institute of International Education maintains a register to help educational institutions in other countries locate faculty members. Applicants register for a fee, providing detailed information about themselves and their interests, and IIE matches their qualifications with overseas requests (See Appendix B for address).

The Israel Aliyah Center recruits teachers at all levels to teach in schools in Israel. The Teacher's Aliyah program is designed to equip the immigrant teacher with the language and an understanding of the Israeli education system. Newly-arrived teachers usually give classes in English as a second language until their command of Hebrew is sufficient to teach their specialty subjects (See Appendix B for address).

Finally, a number of American companies with overseas operations have established schools abroad for the children of their employees. They include Firestone, Mobil Oil, Standard Oil, United States Steel, and others. Consult a business directory for headquarters addresses.

Information about many of the teaching positions described above may be found in *Study and Teaching Opportunities Abroad*. Another valuable source is the Council on International Educational Exchange (CIEE), which assists in planning and operating educational exchange programs sponsored by the more than 165 North American colleges, universities, secondary schools, and educational and religious groups that are members of the Council. It arranges transportation and orientation, completes travel and program arrangements, and provides information and advice on international student travel. CIEE also serves as a clearinghouse for information on worldwide opportunities for study, travel, and work for students and teachers. The CIEE publication, *Whole World Handbook*, is another helpful source of information on teaching opportunities abroad (See Appendix B for address). Other experienced organizations that assist students, teachers and others traveling abroad for educational purposes are the Institute of International Education; the National Association for Foreign Student Affairs, section on U.S. Students Abroad; and the U.S. Department of Education, Office of International Studies (See Appendix B for addresses).

Foreign Language Teaching

Approximately 100,000 people in this country work in the field of foreign language teaching. Over two-thirds teach in junior and senior high schools, and the rest in colleges and universities, elementary schools, and commercial and government-operated language schools. The greatest number teach Spanish, followed in order by French, German, Latin, Chinese, Portuguese and Japanese. In addition, a substantial number teach English to those who speak other languages as their native tongue—Hispanics, Asians, and other ethnic and immigrant groups. The teaching of English to speakers of other languages also offers expanding opportunities for employment abroad in government, academic, and volunteer programs. Still others teach in bilingual education programs, usually at the elementary level, where students whose native language is not English follow a regular academic program in both their native language and English. A large number of bilingual preschool centers also have been established, employing bilingual teachers qualified in early childhood education.

Certification and other requirements

All 50 states and the District of Columbia require public school teachers to be certified by the department of education in the state in which they work. Some states also require certification of teachers in private and parochial schools. In every state the minimum educational requirement for certification is a bachelor's degree, with a specified minimum number of semester hours in education (including a methods course, educational psychology, and student teaching) and in the language (including literature, basic skills, teaching materials, and linguistics). Some states require that the teacher get additional education—usually a master's degree or a fifth year of study—within a stipulated period after initial certification. A prospective teacher who has fulfilled most of the requirements for a teaching certificate is eligible for a provisional certificate in some states. Noncertified personnel may be employed as teachers of foreign languages in elementary schools if they are native speakers of the language or college professors of foreign languages working in experimental programs.

Professors at many community and junior colleges supported by the state or county require certification in foreign languages, which is given by the state board of education; in almost all cases they must also have completed master's degree programs, and, increasingly, doctoral programs. This requirement depends on the laws of each particular state. Professors at four-year colleges and universities are usually expected to have completed or to be completing doctoral programs, including the dissertation, and to continue scholarly research and publication throughout their careers. In certain states highly qualified persons who lack the necessary courses can obtain certification by presenting substantial evidence of their literary, artistic, or scientific accomplishments.

State and local jurisdictions often have general teacher requirements, such as the recommendation of the college, a certificate of health, and United States citizenship. Personal qualifications for public school teachers include a desire to work with young people and the ability to motivate students and relate knowledge to them. Prospective teachers may obtain complete information on educational and general requirements from the state department of education and from the superintendent of schools in each community.

There is usually no citizenship requirement for teaching in private elementary and secondary schools and colleges. There may be a religious requirement in some parochial schools.

In addition to taking required and recommended courses, the future foreign language teacher is advised to get practice in the language by living for a time in a country where it is spoken, if possible. Another excellent means of preparation is residence in one of the "foreign language houses" operated by some colleges and universities; their programs are described in the college catalogues. Training in the use of language laboratory and audio-visual equipment is strongly recommended.

Membership in professional associations is most valuable. These include the American Council on the Teaching of Foreign Languages, the Modern Language Association, the National Education Association, state and local groups, and associations for particular languages.

Employment situation

For a variety of reasons, the job market for foreign language teachers, except in certain less common languages, bilingual education, and TESOL (Teaching of English to Speakers of Other Languages), has become more restricted and more competitive in recent years. At the elementary level there are signs that opportunities will broaden with the introduction of early language training in more schools. In most cases, however, the FLES (Foreign Languages in Elementary Schools) program is unfortunately not yet an integral part of the curriculum. On the positive side, certified elementary school teachers working in FLES programs often receive additional compensation as specialists (plus a transportation allowance, since they must sometimes travel to as many as six or seven schools each day).

High school teachers of foreign language would be well-advised to become certified in two subject areas; two foreign languages or one foreign language plus English are two very marketable combinations. At the high school and college levels, the availability of teaching positions depends on enrollment in foreign language courses. High school foreign language enrollment largely reflects the entrance requirements of colleges and universities, and the situation in this regard has not been encouraging. However, there has been a recent reinstatement of foreign language requirements for graduation from college and for graduate degrees. The dereasing enrollment in foreign language courses is a matter of concern to language educators, of course, but it is to be hoped that those responsible for setting entrance and graduation requirements and for counseling students will also be attentive to the importance of language study for Americans. As a key element of the career education concept, as part of the student's general and essential preparation for life and work, as a means of improving one's skills in English—the study of foreign languages should be given renewed emphasis.

Teachers just out of college may find their opportunities greater if they are willing to accept employment in rural areas, smaller suburbs, or inner-city schools. Private and parochial schools often hire noncertified teachers and may offer smaller classes, but their pay scales are generally lower than in the public schools.

College foreign language teaching is a highly competitive field. College teachers of foreign languages can obtain a complete picture of employment opportunities from the *MLA*

Job Information Lists published quarterly by the Modern Language Association. Each list contains statements from language department chairmen on definite or possible openings at their schools, followed by a list of departments reporting no vacancies. Thus, the job seeker is spared the trouble of submitting useless and expensive applications. Another valuable source of information is the *MLA Guide for Job Candidates and Department Chairmen in English and Foreign Languages.* Write the MLA Job Information Service, 62 Fifth Avenue, New York, NY 10011.

Commercial language schools and those operated by the government—such as the Defense Language Institute and the Foreign Service Institute—usually prefer to hire native speakers as teachers. In the commercial language schools most positions are part-time; there are over thirty such schools in New York City alone.

TESOL

TESOL—the teaching of English to speakers of other languages—is another field that has been expanding significantly. In this country it has taken its place among the full-fledged academic disciplines, with a great deal of literature (such as the *TESOL Quarterly*) and professional interchange. This field also includes the teaching of Standard English as a second dialect. TESOL teachers must undergo a specific training program that includes comparative linguistics, if they are to be certified to teach in public schools. In the absence of qualified TESOL teachers, school districts may grant provisional certification and allow the teacher to earn regular certification while teaching. Positions also exist at the university level, where classes are filled by growing numbers of foreign students attending U.S. colleges and universities.

Cultural centers, YMCA's, and other social service organizations have begun TESOL programs in many areas, and a host of commercial language schools specialize in teaching English to speakers of other languages.

Information about opportunities and specific openings for teachers of English as a second or foreign language may be obtained from the Modern Language Association or from TESOL (Teachers of English to Speakers of Other Languages), the professional organization whose purpose is to promote scholarship, disseminate information, and strengthen instruction and research in this field (See Appendix B for addresses).

Government positions in foreign language teaching

The U.S. Information Agency occasionally hires teachers for its English Teaching Specialist Corps to serve as country or regional English teaching officers, curriculum and materials developers or directors of courses at binational centers. A master's degree in applied linguistics with specialization in teaching English as a foreign language (TEFL) and at least five years of appropriate experience, including one year overseas, are required. Additionally, USIA accepts applications for positions in the Binational Center English Teaching Fellow Program, although actual hiring is done by the local center. This program is open to American citizens with academic training in TEFL theory and methodology; special consideration is given to candidates with an M.A. in TEFL. Most positions are at binational centers in Latin America, though there are occasional requests for fellows in Asia and Africa.

The Peace Corps has openings for teachers of English as a foreign language in Africa, Asia, and Latin America, in the school systems of the host countries at all levels including university. Two or three years' experience is valuable, but not always necessary. Many persons with degrees in English, social studies, and other fields are placed. In this country, VISTA volunteers sometimes teach in bilingual programs.

The Department of Defense employs both foreign and English language instructors at its Defense Language Institutes. The English Language Center located at Lackland Air Force Base, Texas employs English instructors. A number of non-English-speaking members of the United States armed services study English in this country, as do members of allied military forces who will be undergoing technical training at Department of Defense facilities. At the Foreign Language Center in Monterey, California, government employees—both civilian and military—are trained for positions designated as requiring foreign language proficiency. Requirements for instructors include a bachelor's degree or a combination of education and experience and near-native command of the language.

The Department of Defense hires teachers of foreign languages for the Army, Navy, and Air Force Academies in the United States, and elementary and secondary school teachers for its Overseas Dependents Schools.

Further information on the above teaching positions may be obtained from the sources listed in Appendix B.

Other overseas opportunities

Programs abroad sponsored by the U.S. Department of Education and authorized by the Fulbright-Hays Act are for faculty and doctoral dissertation research, group projects and seminars, and teacher exchanges. Special bilateral projects with other nations support short-term institutes, research seminars and exchanges focusing on the study of foreign languages and cultures. Those interested should write the Office of International Education, U.S. Department of Education, Washington, D.C. 20202.

Teachers of Russian who are fluent in the language and also experienced in teaching English may be interested in applying for the USA/USSR Teachers' Exchange Program, which is sponsored jointly by the AFS International/Intercultural Programs and the Soviet Ministry of Education. Overseas and predeparture orientation expenses are paid by AFS; local travel and subsistence expenses in the USSR are covered by the Soviet Government.

The YMCA has openings for teachers of English as a foreign language in Taiwan and Japan. They need college graduates age 21-30, with training and/or experience in linguistics or TEFL.

Information concerning the above programs may be obtained from the sources listed in Appendix B. One of the most useful publications on overseas opportunities for teachers and students is *Study and Teaching Opportunities Abroad* (see page 89 for ordering information.

Chapter 4

LIBRARY SCIENCE

The job of librarians is to make information available to people. Those in user services, such as reference and children's librarians, work directly with the public. Those in technical services, such as catalogers and acquisitions librarians, are concerned primarily with acquiring and preparing materials for use. Librarians generally are classified according to the type of library in which they work: public libraries, school libraries/media centers, academic libraries, and special libraries. About 80 percent of currently employed librarians have some sort of library degree or certification, with the majority having an MLS degree.

The librarian may use foreign language skills in a variety of ways, including book selection, classifying and cataloging, serving users who speak other languages, and working abroad in United States Government libraries, centers, and schools or those operated by other organizations.

Some graduate programs offering a master's degree in library science require that the student have a reading knowledge of at least one foreign language. This is understandable, since almost all libraries—public, private and academic—handle books, reference works and periodicals in a number of different languages in many fields.

Acquisitions librarians select and order books, periodicals, films and other materials that meet users' needs. Classifiers classify these materials by subject matter. Catalogers see to the preparation of cards indicating the title, author, subject, publisher, date of publication, and location in the library. To order and catalog a new book in a foreign language, a librarian must know enough of the language to have a general idea of what the book is about. Bibliographers, who usually work in research libraries, compile lists of books, periodicals, articles, and audiovisual materials on particular subjects. Special collections librarians collect and organize books, pamphlets, manuscripts and other materials in a specific field. Reference librarians answer questions and suggest sources of information that may be useful. They should know at least one foreign language, and preferably more than one, in order to have access to as wide a range of reference materials as possible.

The archives and special collections of some libraries offer opportunities for research and documentation specialists with a strong language background to work in their foreign language collections. For example, one half of the librarians in New York City libraries need foreign language skills. The Jewish Division requires Hebrew and Yiddish. There are also Slavic, German, Romance, and Oriental collections. The African collection requires a variety of African and other languages. Libraries of colleges and universities with foreign language and area studies programs obviously need librarians who can read the relevant languages.

Some librarians work with specific groups of readers. Many libraries in large cities have developed reading and information sections for specific ethnic groups. In addition, some urban libraries offer special programs—such as story-telling sessions and bookmobiles—for Spanish-speaking residents, and need Spanish-speaking personnel to work in these programs with both adults and children.

Not all libraries specifically require prospective employees to know a second language, but nearly all benefit from those who do. And the chances of employment for librarians with language abilities seem to be on the rise. In academic libraries in particular, the expansion or introduction of African, Asian and other area studies programs and the acquisition of related original language materials have increased the need for librarians with skills in less commonly taught languages such as Chinese, Japanese and Arabic. More scientific, literary and philosophical works are coming into the academic library in their original languages. Recognizing these trends, nearly two thirds of the libraries contacted in a survey by the Modern Language Association foresaw an increase in the number of foreign language materials they will purchase and a substantially greater need for language skills in the years ahead.

In addition to the public, private and academic libraries already mentioned, government and other special libraries employ thousands of librarians in the United States and abroad. The Federal Government has been hiring about 150 librarians a year, while others work in state and local government agencies and institutions. Personnel of the Library of Congress in Washington use foreign languages in ordering publications, cataloging, searches, exchanges, and research. Some U.S. Government agencies abroad employ librarians with a knowledge of foreign languages to work in their libraries around the world. The United States Information Agency, for example, has about 200 libraries in more than 95 countries. USIA maintains or supports libraries in cultural centers, reading rooms and binational centers. The Agency's Foreign Service employs professional librarians as regional library consultants. They help plan and implement library programs, train foreign national employees and operate USIA libraries overseas. Applicants must be U.S. citizens and have a master's degree in library science, as well as four years of suitable experience. The Department of Defense also needs librarians with foreign language skills for its Overseas Dependents Schools.

International organizations such as the United Nations, based in this country as well as abroad, have need for librarians fluent in their working languages. Many American companies with overseas interests employ librarians who know foreign languages. Finally, religious and philanthropic bodies employ some librarians in their work abroad.

Further information on library occupations may be obtained from the American Library Association, 50 East Huron Street, Chicago, IL 60611.

Chapter 5

PHYSICAL AND SOCIAL SCIENCES

Physical, Life, and Environmental Sciences

Progress in every facet of American life depends to some degree on our scientific and technical work force. In 1982 about 3 million people—nearly one-fourth of all professional workers—were scientists, engineers, or other scientific and technical workers. But the United States and other English-speaking countries have no monopoly on scientific and technological progress. While English is still in the lead, Russian is now the second most important language of science. A recent survey of articles published in the physical, chemical and biological sciences showed that 70 percent were written in English and about 20 percent in Russian, with the remaining 10 percent primarily in German and French. Indeed, the need to systematize and integrate scientific information and communication processes has created a demand for a new profession: that of the science information and research specialist, combining a knowledge of science, library techniques, and foreign languages. At present there are over 500 science information personnel in Federal Government positions, and the number is expected to increase significantly.

The need for English translations of scientific articles published in foreign languages has led to the development of special facilities and programs for this purpose. For example, the United States Air Force and the Nuclear Regulatory

Commission are using computers to assist in the translation of Russian-language research reports and technical documents in their areas of interest. Large libraries are being maintained to store these documents. But any scientist making extensive use of research materials in chemistry, physics, meteorology, or the biological sciences—all areas in which Russian is the second most frequently used language—would find it advantageous for many reasons to learn Russian rather than depend solely on translations. The time lag between publication and translation, as much as a year or more, is too long for the scientist who must keep up with the latest developments in the field. Furthermore, the number of Russian scientific journals translated into English is small compared to the total number published; many times only abstracts and not full translations are available. The greater a scientist's knowledge of the languages used by foreign colleagues, the more accessible will be the published results of their work.

Joint projects and international scientific conferences and visits also provide opportunities for use of the scientist's language skills. Astronauts and space technicians have found language to be one of the most serious obstacles in carrying out space ventures with the Soviet Union, and joint research in this field is likely to be followed by projects in medicine, ocean exploration, and other areas. Similar scientific and technological projects are bringing Americans together with German, French, and Japanese scientists and engineers. Each year hundreds of international scientific meetings and symposia are held throughout the world, and there is a constant stream of scientists visiting foreign colleagues at their home universities and institutions. The value of all these contacts is greatly enhanced for those with the ability to speak and understand a foreign language.

As American industry becomes increasingly internationalized, so too does its technology. Researchers cannot safely ignore discoveries made in foreign countries, any more than those made in the United States. Thus, private industry is another source of employment for the scientist with training in a foreign language.

Technical writers and abstractors with foreign language skills are being hired by government and industry to help make the rapidly expanding flow of information available to scientists and engineers. Many colleges and universities now offer courses in technical writing; persons in this field organize, write, and edit materials about science and technology in order to establish clearer communication between those who develop information and those who use it. A knowledge of languages can be a valuable asset in technical fields where a substantial body of foreign research is being conducted and reported. Abstractors read books and articles in foreign languages, then prepare summaries or abstracts for the use of scientists. A recent newspaper advertisement sought abstractors with a knowledge of Dutch and Afrikaans, while another firm needed people to prepare abstracts of articles written in French, Spanish, Czech, and Japanese. This work, which requires fluency in the foreign language and good writing ability in English, can often be done part-time or even at home.

Graduate fellowships are available for advanced study abroad leading to master's or doctoral degrees in mathematical, physical, biological, and engineering sciences. The applicant must hold United States citizenship, be a college senior or first-year graduate student, and intend to enroll as a full-time graduate student at a higher education institution. For further information write to the National Science Foundation, Office of Scientific and Engineering Personnel and Education, Washington, D.C. 20550. Exchanges of faculty members and other scholars are sponsored under the Fulbright-Hays Act and other programs; information may be obtained from the Council for International Exchange of Scholars (see Appendix B for address).

Social Sciences

Social scientists study all aspects of human society, from the origins of mankind to the latest election returns. About half work in colleges and universities; a large number work for the Federal Government and private industry. Although many social scientists have traditionally found employment in colleges and universities, the *Occupational Outlook Handbook* foresees little employment growth in the academic sector. Therefore, employment for sociologists, economists, psychologists, and anthropologists will probably increase in applied positions such as evaluation research and program administration. These employment opportunities are found in a wide range of organizations and businesses, including Federal, state and local government agencies, research and consulting firms, health care facilities, labor unions, trade associations, nonprofit organizations, and business firms.

Anthropologists study the human race—its origins, physical characteristics, language, and culture. They often combine research and field work with teaching in colleges and universities, but some work for museums, private industry, and Federal and state agencies. Cultural anthropologists often live with remote or unusual groups of people to learn their ways of life and thus obtain a better understanding of human culture. Obviously, it is essential that the cultural anthropologist be fluent in the language of the people being studied. Other anthropologists specialize in linguistics, the science of language sounds and structure and the historical relationships among languages. Knowledge of several foreign languages is basic to this work. Archeologists study past societies, reconstructing history and culture by excavating and examining the remains of homes, tools, clothing, ornaments, and other evidence. Archeologists, whose work may take them anywhere in the world, should know the past and present languages of the area being studied.

Economists are concerned with the use of resources such as land, raw materials, capital and labor to provide goods and services for society. They analyze the relationships between supply and demand, and how goods and services are produced, distributed, and consumed. Most doctoral programs in economics require a reading knowledge of one or more foreign languages. Economists specializing in international trade, economic development, and international monetary affairs have a particular need for language skills, especially if they plan to work in government or private industry. Many of the government agencies and international organizations discussed in Chapter 2 of this book employ economists in the United States and abroad. Banks, consulting firms, research institutions, and companies with international operations also have need for economists with foreign language competence.

Geographers study the spatial characteristics of the earth. Most are college and university teachers; some combine teaching and research. Whether their particular field is economic, political, physical, or regional geography or cartography, they need foreign languages to study basic literature and to keep up with research abroad. Many foreign books and articles are never translated, while others do not appear in English until long after their original publication.

Historians describe and analyze the past through writing, teaching and research. They generally specialize in the history of a country or region, a particular historical period or an institution. Historians teach in high schools, colleges and universities, but they are also employed by government agencies, consulting firms, archives, museums and private industry. Since historians often specialize in areas other than American history, a knowledge of foreign languages is helpful and often essential in the study of primary source material. Even in the field of American history, the ability to read foreign publications and analyze foreign interpretations of United States policy may be a distinct advantage in both academic and nonacademic careers.

Political scientists study the functions and workings of governments and political organizations—local, national, and international. Foreign language skills are important primarily to those who are concerned with international relations and foreign political systems. They may be teachers, researchers for private, governmental or international organizations, consultants, foreign affairs specialists or advisers, or Foreign Service Officers. In all of these positions, political scientists need a close acquaintance with the history, culture, and language of one or more foreign countries. Otherwise, they will be limited to interpreting world events from the American perspective only, ignoring the cultural differences that underlie political differences. It can readily be seen that in foreign affairs, ignorance of the relevant language can be a serious, perhaps decisive handicap for policy makers and their advisers, who must assess strategic factors, negotiate treaties, and conduct bilateral and multilateral relations. This applies not only to "major" countries such as the Soviet Union, China, and Japan, but to all areas of the world.

Sociologists study the organization and behavior of groups in human society: families, tribes, communities, and governments, along with a variety of social, religious, political and other organizations. In their dealings with immigrant and ethnic groups the ability to speak a foreign language is a great advantage. When carrying out research projects or working in social agencies, sociologists may find themselves seriously hampered if they lack a reading or speaking knowledge of a second language. Increasing numbers of Spanish-speaking sociologists are being employed by state and local government agencies to work with people of Spanish-language background. The study of foreign societies also requires the ability to read the languages involved.

Area studies specialists, who utilize several social sciences in the study of a particular country or region, obviously have an imperative need for language skills. The number of university area studies programs has been increasing rapidly in the past twenty years, covering nearly every part of the world. And employment for area studies specialists is not limited to universities; government and private organizations, for example the Department of State, Library of Congress, Defense Intelligence Agency, and United Nations, also have positions available. A nonprofit organization recently advertised in the *Washington Post* for a specialist in Chinese affairs, seeking a person with good spoken Chinese and a master's degree or doctorate in Chinese studies. The emergence of the Middle East to a prominent place on the world scene has brought with it a need for analysts with a command of Arabic. Area specialists who know Russian, Japanese, French, and Spanish enjoy excellent and expanding opportunities for employment.

Information on individual grants for research in the social sciences and humanities may be obtained from the Social Science Research Council, 605 Third Avenue, New York, NY 10016.

Chapter 6

✓ LAW

Over 600,000 Americans work as lawyers. Most are in private practice, either self-employed or working for other lawyers or law firms. About one-third are employed by Federal, state and local government. Many people who have legal training do not work as lawyers but use their knowledge of law in other occupations—as insurance adjusters, probation officers, legal affairs reporters, or corporate tax experts. In the years ahead the number of law school graduates is expected to increase and intensify the already keen competition for the available jobs.

Knowledge of a foreign language can be a direct, practical asset to the lawyer who works with members of ethnic minority and immigrant groups, does legal aid work, or specializes in international law, maritime law, patent law, or international business. In these fields, lawyers who lack language skills may find themselves dependent on the services of translators and other intermediaries, which can be time-consuming, awkward for both lawyer and client, and in many cases expensive.

There are opportunities, especially in large urban centers, for lawyers with foreign language competence to serve speakers of languages other than English. Among these are immigrants from Mexico, the Caribbean, South America, Europe and Asia. In some cities law student volunteers are assigned to assist civil rights lawyers in protecting the legal rights of such minority groups. Immigration lawyers who handle naturalization and other legal matters for newly arrived immigrants find that knowledge of foreign languages is often useful and even essential. Such lawyers are highly specialized, frequently working with consulates and embassies of foreign governments in connection with residency, employment, and naturalization problems of immigrants.

Lawyers who specialize in international law find that knowledge of one or more foreign languages is invaluable for such matters as settling disputes or breaches of international contracts, counseling on questions of foreign tariff law, and handling cases in foreign and international courts. Those serving corporations with overseas branches or with extensive foreign trade operations may also need foreign language skills when they are involved in obtaining contracts abroad, negotiating trade agreements with foreign executives, or communicating with foreign personnel in American subsidiaries overseas. For instance, a company advertising in the *New York Times* for an international corporate attorney sought a person who "must be able to communicate effectively with both domestic and foreign clientele" and speak either French or German or both. The American office of a German-based corporation considered it important to have "American lawyers who know enough German to represent the patent interests of the company in American courts." A major American law firm recently sought a tax attorney with "knowledge of one or more European languages" to work in its offices abroad. There are also opportunities for lawyers with language skills to work abroad for offices of American corporations or Federal agencies such as the Department of State and the Internal Revenue Service. And international organizations—especially the United Nations and its specialized agencies—employ lawyers with a knowledge of foreign languages on their legal staffs.

Special Note to Students

The usefulness of foreign language study to prospective lawyers is not limited to the fields mentioned above. A recent survey of law school admissions policies showed that most are concerned more with the broad preparation of applicants than with the specific courses and majors they have had in college. They not only accept, but often prefer, students wth a liberal arts education rather than a narrow, strictly "pre-law" background. As an enhancement of a student's ability to use the English language with skill, as well as a direct contribution to his or her knowledge of literature and the humanities, the study of foreign languages can be an excellent preparation for law school.

For further information on careers in the legal profession, write the American Bar Association, 1155 East 60th Street, Chicago, IL 60637.

Chapter 7

MEDIA

Journalism

Newspaper reporters gather information on events which they describe, analyze and interpret for rapid dissemination to large numbers of people. Foreign correspondents, usually experienced reporters, are employed by large newspapers, press services, and news magazines. Other magazines assign members of their staffs or employ free-lance writers for articles with particular appeal to their readers.

Foreign languages are an important asset to employment in journalism. A significant number of newspapers have indicated that foreign language skills are needed in the profession, and that those of their employees are used in varying degrees. In a survey conducted by the Modern Language Association, a newspaper in Florida noted that its editorial department is occasionally required to interview or get a story from a Spanish-speaking person, and many editorial staff members are proficient in Spanish. A newspaper in Delaware stated that speaking and comprehension skills in Spanish can be useful for a reporter with assignments in Spanish-speaking neighborhoods. Several reporters for a newspaper in Louisiana read and speak French, while others know Spanish. As in other professions and occupations, a knowledge of languages spoken by local ethnic groups enhances the reporter's effectiveness. Other practical uses for the journalist's foreign language skills include interviewing foreign visitors and writing up interesting items that appear in foreign newspapers and magazines. Some newspaper publishers have indicated that proficiency in a second language is an important element in the qualifications of a journalist, and that such competence is one of the things that characterize the best kind of newsperson.

Opportunities for employment are offered by publishers of foreign-language newspapers and periodicals, and by press agencies. There are approximately 60 non-English dailies and 300 non-English periodicals in the United States, with a total circulation of over five million. Detailed listings of these publications may be found in the directories of newspapers and periodicals available in public and university libraries. The reader may also consult *Language Resources in the United States: I. Guide to Non-English Print Media*, by Joshua Fishman, National Clearinghouse for Bilingual Education (see Appendix B for address).

Foreign correspondents working for such organizations as the Associated Press and United Press International, and for large newspapers and weekly magazines, have a real need for fluency in foreign languages. Correspondents are hired primarily on the basis of their skills as journalists, and in the past their language skills have often been inadequate or nonexistent. The tide may be turning, though. For example, a major publishing house was recently seeking a staff editor with foreign language skills to cover the international industrial beat. It is now being recognized that the speed and accuracy with which news is transmitted, as well as the reporter's depth of comprehension and ability to judge the authenticity of information, could be improved if the interpreter were not needed.

Schools of journalism are becoming aware of the need for journalists who have an understanding of foreign nations and people. For instance, a master's degree program in journalism at Ohio State University requires students to be fluent in a foreign language, and to spend a six-month internship in the part of the world where they want to be correspondents. The Department of Labor, in its *Occupational Outlook Handbook*, states that persons wishing to prepare for newspaper work should acquire the ability to read and speak a foreign language, in addition to taking courses in English, writing, sociology, political science, economics, and history. To sum up, it appears that there is an increasing demand for journalists with first-rate reporting skills, fluent command of a foreign language, and a good understanding of other cultures and nations.

Staff members of the advertising and circulation departments of newspapers in cities with sizable Hispanic and other ethnic populations may also find a knowledge of foreign languages useful in dealing with advertisers and readers.

Radio and Television

The glamor and excitement of radio and television make broadcasting careers attractive to many people. Over 150,000 workers are employed in broadcasting, besides several thousand free-lance performers and writers, who work on a contract basis for stations, networks and other producers. These media employ staff to produce, write, and direct programs, as well as executives, administrators, technicians, announcers, and performers. Many local networks, both private and public, are increasing their programming for ethnic groups, and Spanish is being introduced more and more on educational television. There are over 300 radio stations throughout the United States that broadcast programs in foreign languages—French, German, Italian, Spanish, and many others. In addition, some stations produce language education programs.

Language skills are needed by program writers and announcers on these stations. For example, in one Maine community with a large French-speaking population, special television programs in French were developed even though the French-speaking residents also speak English. A midwestern network executive stated that foreign language competence is a necessity in specialized areas of programming, and pointed out the desirability of having staff with a knowledge of the cultural and social aspects of the target audience. An American radio station recently advertised for a research analyst fluent in Russian to cover Soviet cultural affairs in Europe. The need for such skills is also evident in international contacts involving the exchange of programs and joint productions with networks abroad. At some stations foreign radio news and other broadcasts are translated into English for rebroadcast or other uses.

Radio and television announcers must be able to pronounce foreign words and names correctly, whether reporting an international sports event, introducing an opera, or conducting an interview with a political leader from abroad; a corps of language experts is not always available.

The Voice of America radio service of the United States Information Agency, which broadcasts in many languages, employs writers, producers, and announcers fluent in those languages. These VOA employees are often responsible for translating English-language news, rendering the script in the style to which the listening audience is accustomed. Others may write foreign-language scripts on American life and culture. Radio Free Europe and Radio Liberty broadcast to countries of Eastern Europe. The use of foreign languages in military intelligence radio broadcasting and monitoring is also very important.

Academic preparation for careers in broadcasting should include courses in English, public speaking, dramatics, and electronics, in addition to foreign language training.

Film

Skills in a second language can help those involved in film production, performance, and technical work, as well as those on the business and administrative side of the film industry. Film production is one of the most international of the arts, in which technical skill and artistic talent transcend national boundaries. Foreign and American film crew members may cooperate on the same film, and American crews frequently do their filming abroad to obtain the authenticity of setting that is so important for visual effects. Some films deal specifically with other cultures and countries: a documentary on problems of migrant workers, a travel film on the sights of Greece, or an educational film that teaches a foreign language. In all these instances, writers, performers, executives, and technicians may need a foreign language in order to have a thorough knowledge of their subject, to communicate with the people being filmed and with each other, to prepare scripts, or simply to get along in the foreign country where they are working.

Distribution of American-made films abroad and importation of films to the United States also provide opportunities for people with foreign language skills. Writing subtitles and dubbing films, which are highly specialized jobs, require a command of the foreign language involved, including its slang and idiomatic expressions. Finally,those interested in film as an art broaden their knowledge of the field and enhance their professional credibility among colleagues when they can understand films in the original language.

Publishing

Positions as editor, editorial assistant, copywriter, proofreader, technical writer, salesperson, and secretarial worker are available in the field of publishing. Foreign language skills are useful for the staffs of many publishing houses, especially those that market their books abroad or publish translations and foreign language textbooks. In a recent *New York Times* advertisement, a major educational publisher sought a totally bilingual (Spanish and English) acquisitions editor with a background in college textbooks and a knowledge of the Latin American educational market. A large book publisher requires foreign languages for its international salespeople, copy editors, and permissions correspondents. Another scientific publisher in Boston was ready to hire a marketing specialist fluent in German, Spanish or French for its overseas trade operations. University presses and textbook publishers need personnel with language competence to work in their editorial, sales, and administrative departments. Even many publishers who do not work regularly with foreign manuscripts or international publishing contracts recognize that their editors need foreign languages as part of their general training. They find that proficiency in a second language is an indication of a broad education and the general ability of a prospective editorial employee. A person who knows a second language is more likely to use his first language well, and facility in English is the skill most needed in publishing.

Thus, the right combination of editorial and foreign language skills will mean better chances for employment in the publishing field.

Chapter 8

TRAVEL AND TOURISM

As the number of foreign visitors to the United States continues to rise each year, industries connected with travel and tourism are increasingly feeling the need for personnel with foreign language skills. In 1983 over 22 million travelers from abroad visited this country, up from 3 million in 1972, and the trend is expected to continue. The reasons for this growth are not only increased prosperity in many countries but also lower fares and the widespread popularity of package tours combining air travel, accommodations, and sightseeing excursions at a cost well within the reach of even less affluent foreigners.

Language has been pointed out as a problem in selling travel in the United States. Foreign tourists need help and services in their own language, and understandably won't come back if they are seriously inconvenienced by a lack of such services. This is particularly true at a time when the strength of the dollar makes the foreign visitor think twice before coming to this country. To help overcome their hesitation, and in an attempt to retain this important segment of the travel industry—which contributed $14 billion to the U.S. balance of trade in 1982—sensitivity to the need for providing foreign tourists with services in their languages is growing.

The National Park Service, for one, is aware of this need, as an estimated 30% of the summer visitors to Bryce, Zion, and Grand Canyon National Parks are from overseas. In the national parks, brochures are available and signs displayed in the major foreign languages. The head of public relations at Yellowstone National Park speaks seven languages, a skill that proved particularly useful the night of an accident involving a group of Italians in one car and Spaniards in the other. According to the Interpretive Specialist for the National Park Service, fluency in foreign languages is especially valued among seasonal staff, who deal with the influx of summer visitors.

The hospitality industries—hotels and motels, resorts, sightseeing companies, restaurants—still fall short of providing adequate multilingual staff and services. Foreign languages are a definite plus in finding employment in this sector. However, the travel industry itself and some other organizations sponsor a number of programs designed to help non-English-speaking tourists overcome the language barrier. The most important program of its kind is operated by the International Visitors Information Service. IVIS maintains a telephone interpreter language bank which can help travelers in over 50 languages. While this bank is staffed by volunteers, one should not overlook the possibilities offered by volunteer work as a means of making contacts through which a paid position might be secured. For Americans traveling abroad, an international assistance program has been introduced at Marriott Hotels through an arrangement with American Express. English-speaking guests will be able to contact the service through the hotel switchboard, and their needs will be interpreted for the hotel staff.

According to the U.S. Travel Data Center, over five million people are now employed in travel and tourism-related industries in this country. The fields in which foreign language skills are needed include:

- Hotels and motels
- Transportation companies (air, bus, rail, ship)
- Tour operators and leaders
- Other tourism-related services

Hotels and motels

Desk clerks, telephone operators, information staff, administrators—all can provide better service to visitors from abroad and enhance their employer's reputation by knowing a foreign language. Hotels and convention centers are becoming more aware of these needs, especially in areas that customarily receive many foreign visitors—New York City, Niagara Falls, Disney World, Washington, the West Coast— but they will continue to grow in other parts of the country as the more adventurous foreigners broaden their travel horizons. This is in addition to the many foreign businessmen who regularly visit Chicago, New Orleans, Miami, Philadelphia, and other industrial and commercial centers. Preference in hiring will undoubtedly go to persons whose foreign language skills help hotels to attract and better serve this growing influx of travelers from abroad—over 24 million expected this year.

Some universities have schools of hotel administration (Cornell is a prominent example), and there are many private training schools in this field. An excellent way of gaining experience in hotel work is to begin as a seasonal employee at a summer or winter resort.

Transportation companies

The international airlines, which schedule hundreds of flights to and from the United States each week, have an obvious need for persons with foreign language skills. Virtually all the personnel of these airlines who deal with the public make use of foreign languages. Flight attendants (stewards and stewardesses), ground hosts and hostesses, flight announcers, information and reservations clerks, and other personnel at international airports who come into contact with foreign travelers are in some cases required to speak a foreign language. In many other cases such skills are recommended or preferred. In addition, employees of domestic airlines serving Puerto Rico and Florida need Spanish for both in-flight and ground duties. Pilots also make use of foreign languages. Salaries are good and there is often the added bonus of reduced-fare vacation flights.

Railroad, bus, and ship lines may also need bilingual personnel both to deal with foreign passengers and to serve Spanish-speaking or other ethnic groups within the United States.

Airlines and shipping companies, as well as some of the larger travel agencies, maintain sales offices in many foreign cities, with Americans employed in managerial or public relations positions; American supervisory personnel are also assigned to foreign airports. As a rule, these companies do not hire specifically for work abroad, but send employees with prior experience in sales, cargo handling, and operations. Knowledge of a foreign language is of course highly useful for an overseas career of this kind and may often serve as one of the criteria for assignment to a position abroad.

Tour operators and leaders

As the influx of foreign visitors to America continues, guided excursion tours will require personnel with language skills. Many such excursions and tours are now being sold as part of package arrangements for tourists from abroad, just as they are for American tourists traveling overseas. There is a need not only for people to accompany the foreign visitors, but also for bilingual guides on sightseeing excursions in cities and to tourist attractions, museum guides, and hosts and hostesses at resorts such as Disneyland, Williamsburg, and the many "theme parks" that have been developed.

Furthermore, there are job opportunities as tour leaders abroad. For instance, positions are available as program leaders for the Experiment in International Living (Brattleboro, VT 05301). Applicants must be at least 21 years of age, and language fluency is required for assignment to French, German, and Spanish-speaking countries. In general, tours originating in the United States are accompanied by a tour operator, who sees to the myriad details that arise in foreign travel. Problems with hotels, restaurants, foreign travel agencies, guides, and even medical emergencies must be handled by the tour operator, the group's liaison with the travel agency arranging the tour. Obviously, fluency in the language and a thorough understanding of the culture are prerequisites for the job.

Those who believe they are qualified for such positions should consult the travel sections of newspapers and write directly to agencies advertising tour programs. They should also keep in mind tours arranged by organizations like college alumni groups, Friends of the Arts in various museums, professional associations and national organizations like the Smithsonian Institution, which has an extensive travel program. For additional information, a helpful publication is the *Whole World Handbook: A Student Guide to Work, Study, and Travel Abroad*. The *Handbook* contains general advice on finding a job abroad, as well as descriptions of employment opportunities. It is available for $5.75 in bookstores or from the Council on International Educational Exchange, 205 E. 42nd St., New York, NY 10017.

Other tourism-related services

Travel agencies dealing extensively with foreign tourists can make use of personnel with foreign language skills. A restaurant manager or captain would find such skills helpful. A recent ad in the *Washington Post* indicated "foreign language is a plus" in the search for a banquet manager. And French-speaking waiters in fine restaurants enjoy well-paid and interesting work. Service companies operating at airports, such as car rental agencies and limousine services, are other possible employers of bilingual staff.

Another fact worth noting is that in many large cities such as New York, Miami, and Los Angeles, a knowledge of Spanish is highly useful for management personnel working with Spanish-speaking employees of hotels, restaurants, and other business establishments.

Special Note to Students

Some areas of special interest to students have already been mentioned, such as the possibility of seasonal employment at resort hotels and tourist attractions and working as a tour leader overseas. For those seeking employment in foreign countries, there are many commercial job placement agencies serving students, and a variety of useful publications such as the *Whole World Handbook*. Highly recommended are the following:

✓ *Study and Teaching Opportunities Abroad: Sources of Information About Overseas Study, Teaching, Work and Travel.* Available for $4.50 from the U.S. Government Printing Office, Washington, D.C. 20402 (Stock No. 017-080-02063-7).

✓ *Student Travel Catalog.* Available for $1.00 from the Council on International Educational Exchange, 205 E. 42nd St., New York, NY 10017.

For jobs overseas, students should be fully informed about the terms of employment, conditions in the country or area concerned, and the extent of the obligation undertaken. They should not travel without sufficient funds and proper arrangements made in advance. The *Student Travel Catalog* mentioned above is an excellent handbook for this purpose.

Chapter 9

SERVICES

Health Services

Health professionals of all kinds—medical students, doctors, nurses, laboratory technicians, medical researchers, hospital administrators, and health educators—are finding more and more that a second language is important, and in some cases essential, in carrying out their work.

Many qualified students have been obliged to go abroad to study medicine because of the limitations imposed on enrollment in American medical schools by the lack of space and funds. In recent years thousands of American students working for M.D. degrees in Europe and Latin America have had to cope with the "language barrier"; some have found that language skills acquired earlier are making a vital contribution to their professional progress. The study of medicine, recognized as one of the most difficult disciplines, cannot be pursued in a foreign school without the requisite knowledge of Spanish, French, German, or Italian. Information on foreign study in medicine may be found in an information sheet "Applying to Foreign Medical Schools," available from the Institute of International Education, Information Services Division, 809 United Nations Plaza, New York, NY 10017. The *World Directory of Medical Schools* contains information about medical schools throughout the world and includes statistics on both national and foreign students studying medicine in a particular country. It is available from the WHO Publications Center, 49 Sheridan Ave., Albany, NY 12210 ($16.25). *Barron's Guide to Foreign Medical Schools* by Carla Fine contains useful background information on foreign medical education. It is available for $4.95 from Barron's Educational Series, 113 Crossways Park Drive, Woodbury, N.Y. 11797. Students wishing information on dental studies abroad should write the Council on International Relations, American Dental Association, 211 East Chicago Avenue, Chicago, IL 60611, for the publication *Dental Schools of the World.*

Laboratory technicians and specialists in medical research need a reading knowledge of the languages in which research reports are written. Russian, German, and French are the most frequently used foreign languages for research material in the biological sciences. The long delays that are common in the published translation of such materials can seriously retard research in these highly specialized fields.

Doctors and nurses are increasingly coming into contact with members of minority groups, new immigrants, and migrant workers who are unable to speak English well enough to describe their symptoms or understand medical instructions. Many hospitals in the United States have hired bilingual personnel and utilized the services of volunteers to deal with these groups, not only in large cities such as Los Angeles, Miami, New York, and Washington, but in many small towns and rural areas as well. A college student in Hanover, New Hampshire volunteered to assist in the care of Spanish-speaking patients at a local hospital, and was soon given a permanent position in the patient services department. A Sunday issue of the *Los Angeles Times* listed openings for bilingual medical personnel: medical assistants, registered nurses, receptionists, an optician, a dentist, a dental assistant, and a hospital housekeeping supervisor. Other major newspapers frequently list openings in health fields where a foreign language is required; recent listings in the *New York Times* included a Spanish-speaking internist, a bilingual dentist and a family practice physician fluent in Arabic.

Positions in the health field are also available overseas, and in most cases require knowledge of the local language. Both the World Health Organization (a specialized agency of the United Nations) and the Pan American Health Organization, which is the Western Hemisphere office of WHO, require public health workers for their programs in developing countries. These organizations need medical personnel with skills in a number of languages, particularly French and Spanish. Intensive language training is often provided before assignment to countries in which less common languages are spoken. CARE, a service organization, recruits doctors, nurses, and laboratory and X-ray technicians for work in Asia, Africa, and Latin America. Qualifications for international employees include a bachelor's or other appropriate degree, some previous overseas experience or certain educational equivalents, and work experience in one or more of the following: nutrition, public health, business administration, agriculture, water resources management, or construction, as well as spoken mastery of a foreign language, preferably Spanish or French. Protestant and Catholic missions require doctors, nurses, health educators, and therapists for all types of hospital, clinic, and rural work. The YMCA has projects in Latin America, Asia, and Europe (See Appendix C for addresses).

Amdoc/Option Agency (3550 Afton Road, Box 81122, San Diego, CA 92138) is a nonprofit personnel service directing health care professionals to areas of need. Short-term and long-term positions are available both in rural America and in developing countries. In many cases, whether it be in a program serving migrant farm workers in Texas, as a surgeon in a small primitive hospital in Haiti, or as a midwife in Sudan, knowledge of a foreign language is essential.

Public health workers are employed abroad by several agencies of the Federal Government. The United States Foreign Service needs nurses for overseas positions; a B.S. degree is desirable. The Department of Defense requires nurses for its Overseas Dependents Schools. The Agency for International Development employs public health specialists in its development assistance programs. And the Peace Corps, with development and education programs in many countries, needs doctors, nurses, nutritionists, therapists, and educators for clinical work and teaching. All of these personnel will find knowledge of a foreign language desirable or necessary. (See Chapter 2 for further information on these government agencies).

Social Work

Social workers assist individuals, families, groups, and communities in using social services to deal with problems such as poverty, unemployment, poor housing, or illness. In cities where there are concentrations of minority groups and immigrants, social workers come into contact with many people who do not speak English. Serving a Puerto Rican family in New York City, Mexican-American farm workers in California, or Latin American immigrants in Miami and other cities, the caseworker cannot establish trust—or perhaps even communicate—without knowing Spanish.

At major ports of entry such as New York, Boston, Los Angeles, and San Francisco, many different languages may be needed by government and private social workers to interview recently arrived immigrants and help them face the problems of their new environment. The New York Association for New Americans, a private agency which assists immigrants, requires caseworkers, counselors, and supervisors with language skills. State and local government service agencies must often provide services to their clients in languages other than English. Community-based agencies and organizations are found in many areas with sizable non-English-speaking groups, and serve these groups in their own languages. For example, a senior citizens' center in Washington, D.C., was recently looking for a Spanish-speaking coordinator. There was another opening for a bilingual counselor at a family planning center. Schools, hospitals and rehabilitation centers may also need bilingual social services personnel, depending on the language groups found in the community.

Religious Organizations

Deciding on a career in religion involves considerations different from those that underlie other career choices; the primary motivation is a strong religious faith and a desire to help others. Nevertheless, it is important for young people to know as much as possible about the profession and how to prepare for it.

Recommended preseminary courses for those planning to become Protestant ministers include foreign languages, in addition to English, history, philosophy, fine arts, music, and religion. Jewish seminaries require Hebrew, and French and German are used in the study of scholarly works by rabbinical students. For the Catholic priesthood, two years of Latin are required, and the study of modern languages is encouraged.

Those pursuing advanced studies in theology need a reading knowledge of classical Greek, and in some cases Semitic and other languages as well.

Within the ministry itself, foreign languages may be an asset. Inner-city churches often have a strong Spanish-speaking contingent. The *Washington Post* recently listed an opening for a bilingual priest to join a ministry team at a home for the aged in Ontario.

In missionary work, knowledge of foreign languages can be crucial. Organizations that send missionaries abroad find it necessary for the majority of their workers to learn one, two, or even three languages in order to minister effectively in the countries to which they are sent. Sometimes, when the languages spoken are rarely taught in the United States, or when different dialects are involved, missionaries are not required to learn the language until they are assigned to a particular area. In such cases the study of any foreign language will familiarize the future missionary with the way languages are learned, an invaluable preparation for a career during which several different languages may be needed.

Other Service Organizations

Many social service organizations need people with foreign language ability, both in this country and abroad. The International Visitors Information Service (IVIS) maintains a booth at Dulles International Airport near Washington to provide information and language assistance to foreign visitors arriving there. Visitors can also telephone the special IVIS language bank to receive help in over 50 languages. Other services provided by IVIS that depend on volunteers' knowledge of a foreign language are a reception and information center, a home hospitality program, multilingual escort and conference services, and scheduling of meetings between international visitors and their professional counterparts. Catholic Relief Services, the YMCA and YWCA, the Red Cross, and other charitable and service organizations sometimes need bilingual workers and volunteers to work with Hispanic and other ethnic groups. Often, caseworkers must deal with people in emergency situations and comprehend their problems, which are complicated by a lack of language skills as well as cultural misunderstandings.

International Voluntary Services (IVS), a private, nonprofit organization, recruits highly trained and experienced volunteer technicians who are skilled in agriculture, public health, engineering, cooperative promotion and other fields relevant to rural development needs. During the two-year period of service, volunteers are provided with living and housing allowances as well as a monthly stipend to be used after IVS service or to help meet other financial obligations. IVS recently had openings in Bangladesh, Bolivia, the Caribbean, Ecuador, Honduras, and Zimbabwe. Most required fluency in Spanish or willingness to learn the local language.

Overseas, the American Friends Service Committee has centers in several countries that conduct programs to promote world peace and social welfare and to provide technical assistance. International assignments require overseas program experience and often foreign language fluency. The Church World Service program of the National Council of Churches of Christ has a limited number of overseas openings each year. Its projects include development programs designed to help people of other countries improve the quality of their lives, and functional programs that provide liaison and agency-building skills along with technical advice on special problems.

The International Liaison, an affiliate of the U.S. Catholic Conference, is a referral center for lay volunteers who wish to serve overseas. It helps volunteers contact programs and agencies according to individual experience, skills and education. Health workers, mechanics, carpenters, secretaries, community workers and others are among those referred to mission programs abroad.

The YMCA is active in many countries, employing Americans in teaching, sports directing, and administration; prior experience with the YMCA in the United States is usually needed. The World Service Workers Program is designed for college graduates with YMCA experience who show marked potential for a professional career in the YMCA. Two-year appointments are available in the Middle East, Africa, Latin America and Asia. Proficiency in Spanish is required for Latin American assignments.

Intercristo specializes in putting job seekers in contact with religious groups which use both paid and volunteer personnel. Approximately 50% of the 30,000 positions they now list are overseas. Although language training may be available prior to beginning missionary work overseas, Intercristo describes language fluency as "a big plus" which boosts one's chances in the selection process. Persons skilled in social services, church and evangelical work, science and technology, education, medicine, mass communications and other areas are among those in demand (See Appendix C for addresses).

For all these positions, and those in which administrators come into contact with local government, the United Nations, and other international bodies, language competence is a necessary or desirable complement to other professional skills.

Chapter 10

INTERPRETING AND TRANSLATING

Interpreters and translators make possible much of the international communication and exchange that takes place in the world, yet relatively little is known of these professions in the United States. Only when a garbled—and often amusing—translation of operating instructions accompanies a foreign-made product, or when the President's interpreter seems to have given an inaccurate rendering of a speech covered by the world press, do they get even fleeting attention. The two professions themselves are often confused: interpreting deals with oral communication, and translation with written materials. The comparatively small number of people working in these fields is another reason for their lack of visibility. Nonetheless, professional translators and interpreters are employed everywhere in the world—by governments, international agencies, conferences, publishers and many other businesses and organizations.

The two skills, though apparently similar, are in reality quite different. A thorough knowledge of the foreign language obviously is essential in each case, but much more is involved. Most translators and interpreters work into their mother tongue; working into the foreign language is much less common. The interpreter must make quick and continuous judgments about what is being said in the foreign (or "source") language, and render it simultaneously or consecutively into the "target" language. There is little or no time to weigh alternatives. The translator, on the other hand, is confronted with a body of written material which must be put into the target language in a clear and faithful representation of the original. There is usually a reasonable period of time to choose among the possible renderings. While the interpreter's mistakes—with rare exceptions—are quickly past, those of the translator remain for later scrutiny. It has been said that the interpreter, who works "in public," is usually an extrovert, and that the less visible translator, who works behind the scenes, tends to be an introvert. In any case, both translators and interpreters need an exceptional command of their native language and at least one—and frequently two or more—foreign languages, a working knowledge of the subject matter (which may be highly technical), good oral or written expression, confidence in their skills, and often a great deal of creativity. More and more, special training is needed by individuals wishing to enter these professions.

Interpreting

Simultaneous interpretation is given idea by idea, or phrase by phrase, as the speaker continues to talk. This technique requires speed and fluency, and is made possible by the use of electronic equipment. Simultaneous interpretation is generally preferred for conferences, and the development of portable equipment has extended its use to other situations. In consecutive interpretation the speaker and the interpreter take turns speaking. A consecutive interpreter must have a good memory, and generally needs to take notes of what is said to be certain to give a complete rendering. Simultaneous interpretation is considered to be more difficult, since the interpreter has no time to make notes but must grasp facts and ideas immediately and accurately.

Conference interpreters serve at international meetings, seminars and discussions. Some are employed as permanent staff members of government agencies and international organizations, while others are hired on a free-lance basis to work at specific conferences. The United Nations has a staff of about 100 interpreters, all of whom are required to know extremely well at least two and preferably three of the official UN languages (English, French, Arabic, Spanish, Russian, and Chinese; German has semi-official status). The next largest group of interpreters in the United States is in the State Department, which has about 20 linguists who are primarily interpreters in its Language Services Division.

International organizations employing interpreters in the United States, in addition to the United Nations in New York, include the World Bank, International Monetary Fund, Organization of American States, Inter-American Development Bank, Pan American Health Organization, INTELSAT, and Inter-American Defense Board. They hire a small number of interpreters on a full-time basis, usually contracting free-lances for specific meetings; all have their headquarters in Washington, D.C. In the Federal Government, the Departments of Justice, Interior, and Defense, as well as State, employ full-time interpreters.

In the free-lance conference interpreting field, experienced interpreters compete for the opportunity to interpret at international meetings on scientific, political, economic, and other subjects. The main languages used at international conferences in the United States are English, French, German, Portuguese, Russian, and Spanish; the demand for Arabic, Japanese and Chinese has increased greatly in recent years.

A number of American interpreters work in Europe, where there are many international organizations, many different languages are spoken, and a large number of meetings are held. However, the market there is highly competitive also.

Escort interpreters accompany visiting delegations or individuals and interpret for them, generally in informal situations. There are more of them than conference interpreters because many more languages are in demand for escort interpreting. The Department of State and private language service agencies are the principal employers of escort interpreters.

Escort interpreters are also becoming more and more important in the area of international business, where they often accompany U.S. businessmen traveling abroad for negotiations. In this capacity they serve not only as linguists but as cultural intermediaries in a broader sense, facilitating international trade. These opportunities are made available either through agencies or through personal contact with firms dealing abroad.

Many cities maintain registries of courtroom interpreters, who are called upon as the need arises. The greatest demand is in Spanish. At present, interpreters for the Federal courts are certified after passing an extremely rigorous examination in English and Spanish. The certifying agency is the

Administrative Office of the United States Courts, Washington, D.C. 20544. Local governments and private organizations also employ interpreters for information centers, hospital work, "hotlines," and other services.

All interpreters must be exceptionally fluent in the language into which they interpret, and their speech must be free of any objectionable accent or impediment. The aspiring interpreter should be well and broadly educated and nearly bilingual; a fairly long period of residence abroad is almost indispensable. But knowledge of languages is only one prerequisite. The other is a genuine aptitude for interpreting, which is not the same as being bilingual. A surprising number of bilingual persons cannot listen to a speech or statement in one language and then repeat clearly and precisely in another language what has just been said—even after taking notes. And simultaneous interpreting requires the additional knack of listening intently to one language while speaking another language at the same time.

Very few schools in the United States provide training in interpretation. Two of the best known programs are those of Georgetown University in Washington, D.C. and the Monterey Institute of International Studies in California. There are several schools of interpretation in Europe and Canada. Further information on training and employment in the field of interpreting may be obtained from The American Association of Language Specialists and in the publications listed at the end of this chapter.

Translating

The translator is required to produce clear, accurate, and well-written renderings of foreign language texts, from general reports and speeches to literary works and highly technical subject matter. This work demands not only a thorough knowledge of the source language, but also the ability to deal with a wide range of materials and to grasp difficult ideas and concepts. Many translators specialize in such fields as finance, patents, life sciences, engineering, poetry and fiction, Bible translation, or children's literature.

As in interpreting, professional translators may work as free-lances or on the staffs of international agencies, government departments, publishing houses, and other businesses and organizations. Many translation agencies and bureaus have been established to meet the growing demand for legal, technical, and business translations; they keep lists of contract translators whom they call upon as needed.

The largest employer of language specialists in this country is the United Nations, which has about 400 translators on its staff in New York. Recruitment is by annual competitive examination and interview. The candidate is required to translate from at least two official languages of the UN into his or her mother tongue, which must be one of the official languages (Arabic, Chinese, English, French, Spanish, and Russian). In addition, all candidates must be graduates of a university where the language of instruction was their mother tongue, and have wide general knowledge. For detailed information write to Office of Personnel Services, United Nations, New York 10017.

The international organizations mentioned in the section on interpreting also employ full-time translators on their staffs. Their requirements are similar, depending on the particular area of interest and the official languages of each organization. See Chapter 2 of this book or the *Yearbook of International Organizations* (available in public and university libraries) for addresses.

In the Federal Government, the Language Services Division of the Department of State employs a sizable staff of qualified linguists, including about 25 translators. The usual range of grades is from GS-9 to GS-11, with reviewers at GS-12. Translators into English are usually required to have a fluent knowledge of at least two foreign languages. Further information may be obtained from the Language Services Division, Department of State, Washington, D.C. 20520.

Other Federal Government agencies employing staff translators include the Central Intelligence Agency, Department of Defense, Department of Commerce, National Security Agency, Department of Justice, United States Information Agency, Department of the Navy, Defense Intelligence Agency, U.S. Army Foreign Service and Technology Center, NASA, the Library of Congress, the U.S. Patent and Trademark Office, and the FBI. See Chapter 2 of this book or the *United States Government Manual* for addresses.

The State Department and many of the international organizations mentioned use the services of free-lance translators for conferences and for work that cannot be handled by their in-house staffs. In most cases a test of the candidate's ability is required. The Joint Publications Research Service (JPRS) of the U.S. Government translates foreign-language articles and other documents for many government agencies, maintaining a roster of contract translators for this purpose. Those wishing to be considered for such translation work should send a resume, indicating languages and fields of specialization, to JPRS, 1000 North Glebe Road, Arlington, VA 22201.

With foreign trade becoming increasingly important to business firms, foreign languages—especially complex legal, technical, and financial terminology—are also coming more into play in private industry. The result has been an explosion in the demand for business and technical translation, using in-house staff, individual free-lances, and specialized translation firms. A German-based pharmaceutical company advertised in the *New York Times* for a German-English translator for its medical affairs department. A Pittsburgh engineering firm needed a French-English translator to work at a construction project in Algeria. Many industrial corporations employ translators at their home offices because they deal with so much foreign-language technical material. And there is another reason why firms are paying more attention to translation: the need to avoid embarrassing or even dangerous errors in meaning or nuance. Obviously, the best defense against error is a translator who knows the current idiomatic use of the language, as well as the subject matter.

Free-lance translators are available to work for any client provided the terms are satisfactory to both, but it is difficult to tap this market as an individual. Translation bureaus, which have grown in number and size, serve as a point of contact between translator and final user. They are called upon by patent lawyers, consulting firms, nonprofit agencies, and many other businesses and organizations to furnish translations in a wide range of fields and languages. They deduct a percentage of the fee and pay the translator directly, often providing reference materials, editing, proofreading, and technical services such as typing and reproduction.

A small number of translators work in the literary field. They are contracted by publishers to translate foreign-language fiction and non-fiction, poetry, and children's literature. Some work for religious organizations on translations of the Bible and other theological texts. Literary translation is generally less well-paid than scientific or technical translation. However, foundation money is occasionally available for these efforts. The National Endowment for the Humanities administers a translation award program. The majority of awards seem to be given for works in the "exotic" languages, which would otherwise go untranslated, although grants for translation from more common languages have also been awarded.

Translators need a broad background of education and experience, since they may be required to translate documents on many diverse subjects. If the translator wishes to specialize, his or her education should include courses in the field of specialization in addition to language training. In the past, all translators learned by trial and error; many entered the profession from other fields. At present, however, a number of schools in the United States and elsewhere offer programs and courses in translation. Lists and descriptions of many such programs may be found in the publications mentioned below.

Those wishing further information on the field of translation should write to the American Translators Association or The American Association of Language Specialists (See Appendix D for addresses).

References

Seleskovitch, Danica, *Interpreting for International Conferences*, 1978.

Survey of Schools Offering Translator and Interpreter Training, ATA Translation Studies Committee, 1983.

Translation and Translators: An International Directory and Guide, ed. Stefan Congrat-Butler, 1979.

Translators and Translations in the Federal Government: A Spot Check, by Ted Crump, 1983.

APPENDIXES

Appendix A

PUBLICATIONS

Applying to Foreign Medical Schools. Institute of International Education, Information Services Division, 809 United Nations Plaza, New York, NY 10017. Free.

Dental Schools of the World. Prepared by the American Dental Association, 211 East Chicago Ave., Chicago, IL 60611.

*How to Get a Job in the Federal Government. Prepared by the Office of Personnel Management. $4.50. Stock No. 017-040-00481-8.

International Jobs: Where They Are and How to Get Them. By Eric Kocher. Addison-Wesley Publishing, 1 Jacob Way, Reading, MA 01867. $6.95

Interpreting for International Conferences. By Danica Seleskovitch. Pen and Booth, 1608 R St. N.W., Washington, D.C. 20009. $10.95

*Occupational Outlook Handbook. Prepared by the Bureau of Labor Statistics, U.S. Department of Labor. $9.00. Stock No. 029-001-02651-0.

Opportunities Abroad for Teachers. International Exchange Branch, Division of International Education, U.S. Department of Education, Washington, D.C. 20202. Free.

Overseas Employment Opportunities for Educators. Department of Defense, Overseas Dependents Schools, 2461 Eisenhower Ave., Alexandria, VA 22331. Free.

Student Travel Catalog. Council on International Educational Exchange, 205 E. 42nd St., New York, NY 10017. $1.00.

*Study and Teaching Opportunities Abroad. Prepared by the U.S. Office of Education. $4.50. Stock No. 017-080-02063-7.

Survey of Schools Offering Translator and Interpreter Training. Prepared by the ATA Translation Studies Committee. American Translators Association, 109 Croton Ave., Ossining, NY 10562. $5.00.

Translation and Translators: An International Directory and Guide. Compiled and edited by Stefan Congrat-Butler. R.R. Bowker Order Dept., P.O. Box 1807, Ann Arbor, MI 48106. $35.00.

Translators and Translations in the Federal Government: A Spot Check. By Ted Crump. Available from the author at 2719 Colston Drive, Chevy Chase, MD 20815 for $2.50.

United States Government Manual. Prepared by the General Services Administration. $9.00. Stock No. 022-003-01099-8.

Whole World Handbook. Council on International Educational Exchange, 205 E. 42nd St., New York, NY 10017. $5.75.

The World Directory of Medical Schools, WHO Publications Center, 49 Sheridan Ave., Albany, NY 12210. $16.25.

Yearbook of International Organizations. Published by the Union of International Associations (available in university and public libraries).

*Publications available from Superintendent of Documents, U.S. Government Printing Office, Washington, D.C. 20402.

Appendix B

1. AGENCIES AND ORGANIZATIONS CONCERNED WITH OVERSEAS TEACHING AND RESEARCH

AFS International Scholarships, 313 East 43rd St., New York, NY 10017

Office of International Relations, National Education Association, 1201 16th St., N.W., Washington, D.C. 20036

Council for International Exchange of Scholars, 11 Dupont Circle, Suite 300, Washington, D.C. 20036

Council on International Educational Exchange, 205 East 42nd St., New York, NY 10017

Commandant, Defense Language Institute, Foreign Language Center, Presidio of Monterey, CA 93940

Institute of International Education, 809 United Nations Plaza, New York, NY 10017

Office of Overseas Schools, Room 234, SA-6, Department of State, Washington, D.C. 20520

Overseas Dependents Schools, Department of Defense, 2461 Eisenhower Ave., Alexandria, VA 22331

Peace Corps, Office of Volunteer Placement, 806 Connecticut Ave. N.W., Washington, D.C. 20526

United States Information Agency, English Teaching Program, 301 4th St., S.W., Washington, D.C. 20547

U.S. Department of Education, Division of International Education, Washington, D.C. 20202

YMCA International Division, 291 Broadway, New York, NY 10007

2. SOURCES OF INFORMATION ON TEACHING OPPORTUNITIES IN FOREIGN LANGUAGES, TESOL, AND BILINGUAL EDUCATION

Defense Language Institute, English Language Center, Lackland Air Force Base, TX 78236

International Schools Services, 126 Alexander St., P.O. Box 5910, Princeton, NJ 08540

Israel Aliyah Center, 515 Park Ave., New York, NY 10022

Modern Language Association, 62 Fifth Ave., New York, NY 10011

National Association for Foreign Student Affairs, Section on U.S. Students Abroad, 1860 19th St., N.W., Washington, D.C. 20009

National Clearinghouse for Bilingual Education, 1555 Wilson Blvd., Suite 600, Rosslyn, VA 22209

TESOL, 202 D.C. Transit Building, Georgetown University, Washington, D.C. 20057

U.S. Department of Education, Office of International Studies, Washington, D.C. 20202

Appendix C

SERVICE ORGANIZATIONS

American Council of Voluntary Agencies for Foreign Service, Inc., 200 Park Ave. South, New York, NY 10003

American Friends Service Committee, 1501 Cherry St., Philadelphia, PA 19102

CARE, 660 First Ave., New York, NY 10016

Intercristo, 19303 Fremont Ave. North, Seattle, WA 98133

International Executive Service Corps, 8 Stanford Forum, Box 10005, Stanford, CT 06904

International Liaison, U.S. Catholic Coordinating Center for Lay Volunteer Ministries, 1234 Massachusetts Ave., N.W., Washington, D.C. 20005

International Voluntary Services, 1424 16th St., N.W., Washington, D.C. 20036

Overseas Personnel Office, National Council of Churches of Christ, 475 Riverside Drive, New York, NY 10027

Pan American Health Organization, 525 23rd St. N.W., Washington, D.C. 20037

YMCA, 291 Broadway, New York, NY 10007

Appendix D

ASSOCIATIONS OF TRANSLATORS AND INTERPRETERS

American Translators Association (ATA)
109 Croton Ave.
Ossining, NY 10562

The American Association of Language Specialists (TAALS)
1000 Connecticut Ave. N.W.
Suite 9
Washington, D.C. 20036

Society of Federal Linguists
P.O. Box 7765
Washington, D.C. 20044

American Literary Translators Association
Box 688, Mail Sta. 1102
University of Texas at Dallas
Richardson, TX 75080

Association of Escort/Interpreters (AEI)
P.O. Box 8093
Washington, D.C. 20024

International Association of Conference Interpreters (AIIC)
14 rue de l'Ancien-Port, CH-1201
Geneva, Switzerland

International Association of Conference Translators (AITC)
Palais Wilson
Case Postale 31, CH-1211
Geneva 14, Switzerland

INDEX
OF
OCCUPATIONS

Abstractor	50, 51
Accountant	9, 15, 28
Accounting assistant	7
Acquisitions librarian	45
Administrative secretary	10
Advertising	7
Agricultural attache	19
Agricultural specialist	17, 28
Airline clerk	67
Airline reservation agent	67
Announcer, radio and television	61, 62
Anthropologist	52
Architect	18
Area studies specialist	54
Astronaut	50
Auditor	9, 15
Bank officer	9
Banking correspondent	9
Bibliographer	46
Bilingual secretary	9, 28, 29, 30, 63
Bookkeeper	10
Broadcaster	61, 62
Budget analyst	15
Business analyst	15, 18
Carpenter	76
Cartographer	52
Cataloger	45
Civil engineer	29
Classifier	45
Clergy	74
Collection agent	10
Commercial loan officer	9
Commercial representative	6
Communications specialist	21
Community development worker	76
Compensation specialist	7
Computer systems designer	8
Consular officer	14
Controller	8
Copywriter	63
Counselor	27, 32
Credit analyst	8

Dental assistant	72
Dentist	72
Desk clerk	66
Doctor	71, 72, 73
Documents certification clerk	9
Economist	15, 21, 24, 28, 29
Editor	28, 63
Editorial assistant	63
Education administrator	32
Education specialist	27, 28, 73
Electronics engineer	8
Electronics technician	20
Engineer	8, 21, 28
Executive secretary	9
Export manager	7
Film producer	61, 62
Financial analyst	15, 28, 29
Financial director	8
Financial officer	7
Flight attendant	67
Foreign Commercial Service officer	19
Foreign correspondent	59, 60
Foreign Service Officer	14, 16
Freelance writer	61
Geographer	52
Geologist	21
Guide	16, 68
Health educator	71
Health worker	18, 30, 71-73, 76
Historian	53
Home economist	27
Hospital administrator	71
Hospital worker	72
Hotel administrator	66
Hotel information clerk	66
Housekeeping supervisor	72
Immigration officer	24
Information officer	15
Insurance agent	7
International broadcaster	17
Interpreter	15, 28, 29, 79-82
Journalist	59-61

Laboratory technician   8, 71
Law enforcement officer   23
Lawyer   15, 16, 18, 24, 29, 55-57
Librarian   25-26, 28, 45-47
Loan officer   15, 29

Marketing coordinator   7
Media executive   61
Media performer   61
Media technician   61
Medical assistant   72
Medical researcher   71, 72
Meteorologist   20, 21
Missionary   76-77

National Park Service officer   65-66
Newspaper reporter   59
Nurse   71, 72, 73
Nutritionist   73

Optician   72

Peace Corps volunteer   17, 35
Personnel manager   7
Personnel officer   14
Police officer   27
Political scientist   53
Production engineer   8
Production manager   7
Program writer   61
Project analyst   29
Public health specialist   73
Public information officer   28
Publishing   63
Purchasing agent   7

Quality control supervisor   8

Radio and television announcer   61, 62
Realtor   7
Receptionist   10
Reporter   59-60
Research scientist   20
Researcher   8, 21, 26, 71
Restaurant captain   69
Restaurant manager   69

Sales engineer 7
Sales representative 7, 63
School counselor 32
Scientific information specialist 49
Scientist 50, 51
Secretary 9-10, 28, 63, 76
Service organization volunteer 75-77
Social worker 73-74
Sociologist 53
Space technician 50
Special collections librarian 46
Statistician 20, 24, 28, 29
Stenographer 9-10
Switchboard operator 10
Systems analyst 7

Teacher 16, 18, 33-43

Technical writer 8, 50, 63
Telephone operator 66
Telex/telegraph engineer 8
Therapist 73
Tour operator (guide) 68
Translator 15, 21, 28, 29, 79-80, 82-85
Transport equipment specialist 8
Transportation company sales agent 67-68
Travel specialist 20
Typist 10

VISTA volunteer 18